Fundamentalism: A Very Short Introduction

VERY SHORT INTRODUCTIONS are for anyone wanting a stimulating and accessible way in to a new subject. They are written by experts, and have been published in more than 25 languages worldwide.

The series began in 1995, and now represents a wide variety of topics in history, philosophy, religion, science, and the humanities. Over the next few years it will grow to a library of around 200 volumes – a Very Short Introduction to everything from ancient Egypt and Indian philosophy to conceptual art and cosmology.

- Very Short Introductions available now:

ANARCHISM   Colin Ward
ANCIENT EGYPT   Ian Shaw
ANCIENT PHILOSOPHY
   Julia Annas
ANCIENT WARFARE
   Harry Sidebottom
ANGLICANISM   Mark Chapman
THE ANGLO-SAXON AGE
   John Blair
ANIMAL RIGHTS   David DeGrazia
ARCHAEOLOGY   Paul Bahn
ARCHITECTURE
   Andrew Ballantyne
ARISTOTLE   Jonathan Barnes
ART HISTORY   Dana Arnold
ART THEORY   Cynthia Freeland
THE HISTORY OF
   ASTRONOMY   Michael Hoskin
ATHEISM   Julian Baggini
AUGUSTINE   Henry Chadwick
BARTHES   Jonathan Culler
THE BIBLE   John Riches
THE BRAIN   Michael O'Shea
BRITISH POLITICS
   Anthony Wright
BUDDHA   Michael Carrithers
BUDDHISM   Damien Keown
BUDDHIST ETHICS
   Damien Keown
CAPITALISM   James Fulcher
THE CELTS   Barry Cunliffe

CHOICE THEORY
   Michael Allingham
CHRISTIAN ART   Beth Williamson
CHRISTIANITY   Linda Woodhead
CLASSICS   Mary Beard and
   John Henderson
CLAUSEWITZ   Michael Howard
THE COLD WAR   Robert McMahon
CONSCIOUSNESS   Susan Blackmore
CONTEMPORARY ART
   Julian Stallabrass
CONTINENTAL PHILOSOPHY
   Simon Critchley
COSMOLOGY   Peter Coles
THE CRUSADES
   Christopher Tyerman
CRYPTOGRAPHY
   Fred Piper and Sean Murphy
DADA AND SURREALISM
   David Hopkins
DARWIN   Jonathan Howard
THE DEAD SEA SCROLLS
   Timothy Lim
DEMOCRACY   Bernard Crick
DESCARTES   Tom Sorell
DESIGN   John Heskett
DINOSAURS   David Norman
DREAMING   J. Allan Hobson
DRUGS   Leslie Iversen
THE EARTH   Martin Redfern
EGYPTIAN MYTH   Geraldine Pinch

For more information visit our web site
www.oup.co.uk/general/vsi/

Malise Ruthven

FUNDAMENTALISM

A Very Short Introduction

OXFORD
UNIVERSITY PRESS

OXFORD

UNIVERSITY PRESS

Great Clarendon Street, Oxford OX2 6DP

Oxford University Press is a department of the University of Oxford.
It furthers the University's objective of excellence in research, scholarship,
and education by publishing worldwide in

Oxford New York

Auckland Cape Town Dar es Salaam Hong Kong Karachi
Kuala Lumpur Madrid Melbourne Mexico City Nairobi
New Delhi Shanghai Taipei Toronto

With offices in

Argentina Austria Brazil Chile Czech Republic France Greece
Guatemala Hungary Italy Japan Poland Portugal Singapore
South Korea Switzerland Thailand Turkey Ukraine Vietnam

Oxford is a registered trade mark of Oxford University Press
in the UK and in certain other countries

Published in the United States
by Oxford University Press Inc., New York

First edition published as an Oxford University Press Paperback in 2005
New edition published as a Very Short Introduction 2007

British Library Cataloguing in Publication Data

Data available

Library of Congress Cataloging in Publication Data

Data available

Typeset by RefineCatch Ltd, Bungay, Suffolk
Printed in Great Britain by
Ashford Colour Press Ltd., Gosport, Hampshire

ISBN 978-0-19-921270-5

3 5 7 9 10 8 6 4 2

Contents

Preface

This book is the fruit of several years' reflection about the revivals
that seem to be occurring in all the major religious traditions and
the capacity these revivals have for generating highly charged social
and political conflicts in a shrinking globalized world where people
of differing and competing faiths are having to live in close
proximity with each other. While recognizing that fundamentalism
is a fact of life in the 21st century – one that was illustrated in the
most spectacular way on 11 September 2001 – this introduction
seeks to untangle some of the meanings associated with the term,
despite its obvious drawbacks.

Fundamentalism originated in the very specific theological context
of early 20th-century Protestant America, and its applicability
beyond its original matrix is, to put it mildly, problematic.
Nevertheless, as I hope to show through numerous examples and
parallels, there are compelling family resemblances between
militancies or fundamentalisms in different religious traditions.
They may not add up to a coherent ideological alternative to the
triumph of liberal democracy as described by Francis Fukuyama in
his celebrated 1992 essay *The End of History and the Last Man*. But
they are symptomatic, I believe, of the spiritual dystopias and
dysfunctional cultural relationships that characterize the world of
what some contemporary commentators are choosing to call 'Late
Capitalism'.

Many people, students, friends, and colleagues, contributed to this book during its gestation. Students at Dartmouth College, Aberdeen University, the University of California, San Diego, and at the Colorado College helped to focus my thinking with their questions and essays. Academic friends and colleagues, including the late Jim Thrower, the late Albert Hourani, Hans Penner, Gene Garthwaite, Philip Khoury, Arthur Droge, Robert Lee, Charles Tripp, Sami Zubaida, Max Taylor, David Weddle, Ketil Volden, Efraim Inbar, and Fred Halliday, helped stimulate my thinking by inviting me to conferences, lectures, and seminars. I would like to express my thanks to them all, and to Martin Marty and Scott Appleby for inviting me to two meetings of the Fundamentalism Project in Chicago in 1990 and 1993 which first aroused my interest in the subject and gave me the opportunity to meet and talk with scholars from several disciplines and countries.

Elfi Pallis kindly supplied some of the information on Jewish fundamentalism that appears in Chapter 6.

List of illustrations

The publisher and the author apologize for any errors or omissions in the above list. If contacted they will be pleased to rectify these at the earliest opportunity.

Chapter 1
Family resemblances

'Heave an egg out of a Pullman window', wrote H. L. Mencken, the famous American journalist, in the 1920s, 'and you will hit a Fundamentalist almost anywhere in the United States today'. 'Fundamentalism' is a word with which everyone is familiar now. Hardly a day passes without news of some terrorist atrocity committed by religious militants or fundamentalists in some part of the world. On 7 July 2005 an acquaintance was actually reading this book on the London Underground, when a nearby carriage exploded, killing dozens of commuters in the worst-ever terrorist atrocity committed on British soil. Altogether, the suicide bombers – three young British Muslim men from Leeds – succeeded in killing 53 people in addition to themselves, while wounding hundreds more, many of whom will be maimed for life.

'The fact that I was reading your book when the bomb went off on the train profoundly conditioned my thoughts in retrospect about that experience, and much else besides', Jonathan Williams, a curator at the British Museum, would later write in an e-mail.

> Crucially, it allowed me to realize that whatever the motive cause
> was that drove these young men to kill themselves and take too
> many others with them, the key context where we need to look for
> understanding is not 'Islam', but the failure of traditional religion to
> encompass modernity.

My views on lots of things have changed in consequence – the exclusive truth claims of my own Christian religion for instance, which I am still struggling with, and more parochial matters like the Anglican Communion's utterly distasteful obsession with issues of sexual orientation.

The most spectacular fundamentalist atrocity of all was the suicide hijacking on 11 September 2001 of three airliners by Islamist militants belonging to the al-Qaeda network, whose titular head is the Saudi dissident Osama bin Laden. Nearly 3,000 people were killed when the planes crashed into the World Trade Center in New York and the Pentagon near Washington. The atrocity was a classic example of the 'propaganda of the deed': the image of imploding towers, symbols of Western capitalism, has been etched into public consciousness as an icon of Islamist terror or resistance to American hegemony, according to one's point of view. But there have been dozens of other atrocities blamed on fundamentalists which have caught the headlines.

1. The World Trade Center, 9/11

Most of them have been attributed to Muslim terrorists whose hostility to the West, and to the United States in particular, is widely presumed to be the outcome of their fundamentalist views. Though far from being exclusive to Islam – Jewish, Sikh, and Hindu extremists have been responsible for assassinating three prime ministers – the world of Islam seems particularly prone to religiously inspired violence at this time.

Foremost among the conflicts attributable to fundamentalist intransigence is the Arab-Israel dispute, still the world's most dangerous flashpoint. For the rationally minded person, whatever their religious background, the Middle East impasse illustrates the pitfalls into which fundamentalist politics is driving the world. Monotheists (who include most Jews, Christians, and Muslims) may worship the same single transcendental deity, whether known by the name of Jehova, the Trinity, or Allah ('The God' as Muslims know Him). But when it comes to understanding His will, or intentions, His self-proclaimed followers invariably adopt opposing standpoints. For the secular non-believer, or for the liberal believer who takes a sophisticated view of religious discourse, the god of fundamentalism must be mischievous, if not downright evil, a demonic power who delights in setting humans at each other's throats.

Religious fundamentalism, as it is broadly understood, has been a major source of conflict since the late 1980s and early 1990s, when the Berlin Wall came down and the Soviet Union collapsed, bringing the Cold War to an end with its attendant spin-offs in Asia, Africa, and Latin America. The death-toll from modern religious conflicts, or conflicts involving religion, is formidable. Not all these conflicts, perhaps, can be laid at the door of religious fundamentalism. Local factors, including ethnicity and nationalism, come into the picture. But religion, as a source of motivation and identity, seems to have replaced the old ideologies of Marxist-Leninism, national socialism, and anti-colonialism as the principal challenge to a world order based on the hegemonic power of the liberal capitalist West. Just as the contradictions within liberalism (for example, between the universal rights of man and the pursuit of imperial trade) gave rise to the anti-colonial movements of the post-Second World War era, so the earliest shoots of fundamentalism (semantically, if not as an age-old phenomenon) came to fruition in the United States in the very heart of the capitalist West.

Academics are still debating the appropriateness of using the F-word in contexts outside its original Protestant setting. Islamic scholars argue that since all observant Muslims believe the Koran, the divine text of Islam, to be the unmediated Word of God, all are committed to a doctrine of scriptural inerrancy, whereas for Protestants biblical inerrancy is one of the hallmarks that distinguishes fundamentalists from liberals. If all believing Muslims are fundamentalists in this sense of the word, then the term is meaningless, because it fails to distinguish between the hard-edged militant who seeks to Islamize his society and the quietist who avoids politics completely. Higher criticism of the Bible, based on close textual study – the original cause of the Protestant fundamentalist revolt against liberalism and modernism – challenged traditional teachings by claiming, for example, that the Book of Isaiah has more than one author and that the Pentateuch, the first five books of the Old Testament, was not authored by Moses himself. Higher criticism of the Koran, by contrast, which would challenge the belief that every word contained in the text was dictated to Muhammad by God through the agency of the Angel Gabriel, has not been a major issue in the Muslim world to date, though it may become so in due course, as literary-critical theories gain ground in academic circles. The present concerns of most Muslim fundamentalists are largely of a different order: the removal of governments deemed corrupt or too pro-Western and the replacement of laws imported from the West by the indigenous Sharia code derived from the Koran and the *sunna* (custom) of the Prophet Muhammad. On slightly different grounds, scholars of Judaism point out that 'fundamentalist' is

4

much too broad a term when applied both to ultra-orthodox groups known as Haredim (some of whom refuse to recognize the legitimacy of the State of Israel) and the religious settlers of Gush Emunim (the Bloc of the Faithful) who place more emphasis on holding on to the Land of Israel than on observing the Halakha (Jewish law).

Fundamentalism, according to its critics, is just a dirty 14-letter word. It is a term of abuse levelled by liberals and Enlightenment rationalists against any group, religious or otherwise, that dares to challenge the absolutism of the post-Enlightenment outlook. Other scholars argue that fundamentalism is a caricature or mirror-image of the same post-Enlightenment outlook it professes to oppose: by adopting the same rational style of argument used by the secular enemy, fundamentalists repress or bleach out the multifaceted, polysemic ways in which myth and religions appeal to all aspects of the human psyche, not just to the rational mind, with fundamentalists exposing what one anthropologist calls 'the hubris of reason's pretence in trying to take over religion's role'.

Words have a life and energy of their own that will usually defy the exacting demands of scholars. The F-word has long since escaped from the Protestant closet in which it began its semantic career around the turn of the 20th century. The applications or meanings attached to words cannot be confined to the context in which they originate: if one limits fundamentalism to its original meaning one might as well do the same for words like 'nationalism' and 'secularization' which also appeared in the post-Enlightenment West before being attached to movements or processes in non-Western societies. Whatever technical objections there may be to using the F-word outside its original sphere, the phenomenon (or rather, the phenomena) it describes exists, although no single definition will ever be uncontested. Put at its broadest, it may be described as a religious way of being that manifests itself in a strategy by which beleaguered believers attempt to preserve their distinctive identities as individuals or groups in the face of modernity and secularization.

Bruce Lawrence, a scholar who believes that the F-word *can* be extended beyond its original Protestant matrix, sees the connection with modernity as crucial: fundamentalism is a multifocal phenomenon precisely *because* the modernist hegemony, though originating in some parts of the West, was not limited to Protestant Christianity. The Enlightenment influenced significant numbers of Jews, and because of the colonization of much of Africa and Asia in the 19th and early 20th centuries, it touched the lives and destinies of many Muslims. In his view, the modernist hegemony did not end with the attainment of political independence by so-called Third World countries. Indeed, given the far-reaching consequences of the scientific revolution that flowed from the Enlightenment, the modern predicament against which fundamentalists everywhere are reacting has been extended to every corner of the planet.

Rather than quibbling about the usefulness of fundamentalism as an analytic term, I propose in this book to explore its ambiguities, to unpack some of its meanings. The word may be less than satisfactory, but the phenomena it encompasses deserve to be analysed. Whether or not we like the term, fundamentalist or fundamentalist-like movements appear to be erupting in many parts of the world, from the Americas to South-East Asia. No one would claim that these movements, which occur in most of the world's great religious traditions, are identical. But all of them exhibit what the philosopher Ludwig Wittgenstein called 'family resemblances'. In explaining his analogy, Wittgenstein took the example of games: board games, card games, ball games, Olympic Games, and so forth. Instead of assuming that all must have a single, defining feature because of the common name applied to them, games should be examined for similarities and relationships. Such an examination would reveal a complicated network of features that criss-cross and overlap: sometimes overall similarities, sometimes similarities of detail such as one finds in different

members of the same family, in which build, features, colour of eyes, gait, and temperament criss-cross and overlap in the same way.

Before proceeding to explore these resemblances, it would be useful to recapitulate the history of the F-word and its burgeoning semantic career. Its origins are quite revealing. Although the word has acquired negative connotations in much of the world, it did not begin as a term of abuse or even criticism. It appeared early in the 20th century not, as might have been expected, in the Bible Belt of the Old South, but in southern California, one of America's most rapidly developing regions (in the same area and at about the same time that one of fundamentalism's principal bug-bears, the Hollywood film industry, made its appearance). In 1910 Milton and Lyman Stewart, two devout Christian brothers who had made their fortune in the California oil business, embarked on a five-year programme of sponsorship for a series of pamphlets which were distributed free of charge to English-speaking Protestant pastors, evangelists, missionaries, theological professors, theological students, YMCA secretaries, Sunday School superintendents, religious lay workers, and editors of religious publications throughout the world. Entitled *The Fundamentals: A Testimony of Truth*, the tracts, written by a number of leading conservative American and British theologians, were aimed at stopping the erosion of what the brothers and their editors considered to be the fundamental beliefs of Protestant Christianity: the inerrancy of the Bible; the direct creation of the world, and humanity, *ex nihilo* by God (in contrast to Darwinian evolution); the authenticity of miracles; the virgin birth of Jesus, his Crucifixion and bodily resurrection; the substitutionary atonement (the doctrine that Christ died to redeem the sins of humanity); and his imminent return to judge and rule over the world.

Like many conservative American Protestants, technically known as premillennial dispensationalists, the Stewart brothers believed that the End Times prophecies contained in the Old Testament books of Ezekiel and Daniel, and the Revelation of St John, the last book of the New Testament, refer to real (not symbolic) events that will soon take place on the plane of human history. Drawing on a tradition of prophecy interpretation developed by an Anglo-Irish clergyman, John Nelson Darby (1800–82), they argued that since many Old Testament prophecies about the coming Messiah were fulfilled with the coming of Christ as documented in the New Testament, other predictions, concerning the End Times, will soon come to pass. Expecting the world to end at any moment, they saw it as their duty to save as many people as possible before the coming catastrophe, when sinners would perish horribly and the saved would be raptured into the presence of Christ.

Being successful businessmen, the Stewarts wanted, and expected, results. As Lyman wrote to Milton after learning that the American Tobacco Company was spending millions of dollars distributing free cigarettes in order to give people a taste for them: Christians should 'learn from the wisdom of the world'. Theological motives were complemented by business competition. Lyman's principal agenda in the oil business was fighting his rival John D. Rockefeller's attempts to monopolize the industry. It may or may not be coincidental that one of the first preachers he hired came to his attention after preaching against 'something that one of those infidel professors in Chicago University had published'. Chicago Divinity School, a hotbed of liberalism, had been founded and endowed by John D. Rockefeller.

Some three million copies of *The Fundamentals* were circulated, on both sides of the Atlantic. The *-ist* was added in 1920 by Curtis Lee Laws, a conservative Baptist editor: Fundamentalists, he declared, were those who are ready to do battle royal for The Fundamentals. About half the American contributors to *The Fundamentals*, including such leading lights as Reuben Torrey and Cyrus Ignatius Scofield, were premillennialists. Before endowing *The Fundamentals*, Lyman Stewart had been a major sponsor of Scofield's Reference Bible, first published in 1909, and still the preferred commentary of American premillennialists.

The belief that Jesus would return to rule over an earthly kingdom of the righteous after defeating the Antichrist dates back to the earliest phase of Christianity, when the apostles lived in the daily expectation of his return. Dismayed by its revolutionary potential, which challenged the renovated imperial cults, common to both Eastern Orthodoxy and Western Catholicism, that conferred divine legitimacy on the Holy Roman and Byzantine emperors, the early church fathers, notably St Augustine (354–430) allegorized and spiritualized the coming Kingdom of God. Christian apocalyptic became part of the everyday fabric of Christian life and belief, and to that extent reinforced eschatological awareness by embedding it in liturgy and preaching while distancing Catholic thought from literalistic readings of prophecy, and especially notions of an earthly millennium. The seal on Augustine's teaching was set by the Council of Ephesus in 431 which condemned millennialism and expurgated works of earlier church fathers thought to be tainted with the doctrine. After the Reformation loosened the Church's grip on Christian teaching, millennialist ideas resurfaced in such apocalyptic movements as the Anabaptists of Münster in Germany and Fifth Monarchy Men who took part in the English Revolution. Transplanted to America, where constitutional separation of church and state encourages religious innovation, millennialist ideas took root in fertile soil.

The number of premillennialist Protestants (who believe that the Second Coming will be followed by the thousand-year reign of Christ on earth) has been estimated conservatively at eight million. Most American fundamentalists are premillennialists, although there are many variations in their approaches to the Second Coming: many of them, in the course of time, have actually become postmillennialists, who argue that the world must be put to rights by people *before* Jesus's return. In no tradition does one find a complete consensus about what the fundamentals of the faith really are. Fundamentalists are nothing if not selective about the texts they use and their mode of interpretation. They are also much more innovative in the way they interpret the texts they select than is often supposed. In this respect they may be contrasted with traditionalists.

'Tradition', like 'fundamental', can be understood in more than one way. Among Roman Catholics, Anglicans, and other religious communities, the word conveys the sense of a cumulative body of ritual, behaviour, and thought that reaches back to the time of origins. In Catholicism especially, tradition embodying the accumulated experience and knowledge of the Church is seen as a source of authority equal to scripture. Tied to the exclusive authority of the Church, tradition was affirmed at the Council of Trent (1545–63), the Church's official response to the challenge posed by the *sola scriptura* doctrine of the Protestant reformers.

In the Islamic tradition similar considerations apply: tradition here means the accumulated body of interpretation, law, and practice as developed over the centuries by the *ulama*, the class of learned men who constitute Islam's professional class of religionists or clerics. Throughout Islamic history there have been renovators or reformers who, like Luther, challenged the authority of the *ulama* on the basis of their readings of the Sources of Islam, namely the Koran and the Hadiths – the latter, sometimes confusingly translated as 'Traditions', are canonized reports about Muhammad's deeds and teachings, based, it is supposed, on the oral testimony of his contemporaries and passed down by word of mouth before being collated into written collections. In this sense, the medieval scholar Ibn Taymiyya (d. 1326), who ended his life in prison for challenging the authority of the *ulama* and rulers of his day, was a fundamentalist. Significantly, his writings are extremely popular among today's Islamist militants.

A less specialized meaning of tradition, however, is also relevant here. In a broader context, tradition is simply what occurs unselfconsciously as part of the natural order of things, an unreflective or unconsidered *Weltanschauung* (world view). In the words of Martin Marty, most people who live in a traditional culture do not know they are traditionalists. Tradition, in this sense, consists in not being aware that how one believes or behaves is traditional, because alternative ways of thinking or living are simply not taken into consideration. In traditional societies, including the mainly rural communities that formerly constituted the American Bible Belt, the Bible was seen as comprehensively true, a source of universal wisdom, knowledge, and authority deemed to have been transmitted to humanity by God through the prophets, patriarchs, and apostles who wrote the Bible. The latter was not thought of as a scientific textbook; but nor did the ordinary pastor or worshipper consider it unscientific. For most of the 18th and 19th centuries, the Bible was considered compatible with reason, or at least with that version of reason conveyed by the common-sense philosophy which spread to North America from Scotland, along with Calvinist theology and more or less democratic forms of church governance.

When Higher Criticism, originating in Germany, began to challenge the received understandings of the Bible, for example by using sophisticated methods of textual analysis to argue that books attributed to Moses or Isaiah show evidence of editorial changes, textual accumulations, and multiple authorship, or that the doctrine of the virgin birth of Christ depended on a mistranslation of the original Greek text, unreflective tradition (the received knowledge of generations) was converted into reactive defensiveness. From this perspective, fundamentalism may be defined as tradition made self-aware and consequently defensive. In Samuel Heilman's words, traditionalism is not fundamentalism, but a necessary correlate to it:

> In all religions, but especially in Protestantism, the active defence of tradition demands selectivity, since the text of the Bible is too vast and complex to be defended in all its details.

Like any military commander, the fundamentalist had to choose the ground on which to do battle royal with the forces of liberalism and Higher Criticism. *The Fundamentals* was part of the process that galvanized this reaction. In America it split the more democratically organized denominations, including Presbyterians, Baptists, Lutherans, and Methodists, generating bitter culture-wars inside their churches. In most of the American denominations it represented the grass-roots reaction to the elitism of the seminaries, perceived as being out of touch with the culture and beliefs of ordinary believers. Yet, as Marty and Appleby point out, the very idea behind the project revealed the distance that had already been travelled along the path of secularity: designating 'fundamentalisms' automatically places the designator at a considerable remove from the time when religion thrived as a total way of life. To identify any one thing or set of beliefs or practices as essential is to diminish other elements of what was once an organic whole.

The most famous of the battles royal which tore many American churches apart in the first half of the 20th century was the Monkey Trial in Dayton, Tennessee in 1925. As Garry Wills, one of America's best-known commentators, has explained, the trial was something of a put-up job, engineered, in effect, by the American Civil Liberties Union (ACLU) to challenge an obscure and little-used Tennessee state law banning the teaching of evolution in schools.

Many Southern states had such laws early in the 20th century. A biology teacher, John Scopes (who subsequently admitted that he had missed teaching the classes dealing with evolution), claimed (rather shakily) to have broken the law. It was an early example of what would later be known as a media event, in which the coverage itself was more important than what actually occurred in court. Hundreds of journalists attended, including the most famous reporter of the day, H. L. Mencken of the *Baltimore Sun*. Radio lines were brought into the courtroom, and the judge held up proceedings to allow photographers to get their shots. The fundamentalist defenders of the state law won the trial on points. With a fundamentalist jury, three members of which testified that

Opposing Christian views of evolution

1. ANTI

All the ills from which America suffers can be traced back to the teaching of evolution. It would be better to destroy every other book ever written and save just the first three verses of Genesis.

> (William Jennings Bryan, in Vincent Crapanzano, Serving the Word:
> Literalism in America from the Pulpit to the Bench)

Evolution is the root of atheism, of communism, nazism, anarchism, behaviorism, racism, economic imperialism, militarism, libertinism, anarchism, and all manner of anti-Christian systems of belief and practice.

> (Henry Morris, The Remarkable Birth of Planet Earth)

2. PRO

Evolutionary theory emphasizes our kinship with nonhuman animals and denies that we were created separately. But it does not interfere with the central Judaeo-Christian message that we are objects of special concern to the Creator. It simply denies us an exclusive right to that title.

> (Philip Kitcher, Abusing Science: The Case against Creationism)

they read nothing but the Bible, the verdict was a foregone conclusion. The state law was upheld, but Scopes had his conviction quashed on appeal, which prevented the ACLU from pursuing its original aim of bringing the case to a higher federal court. He went on to become a geologist after winning a scholarship to the University of Chicago.

2. The Scopes trial, Dayton, Tennessee, 1925

Culturally, the media battle was a devastating defeat for fundamentalism. In a famous cross-examination before the trial judge, William Jennings Bryan, former secretary of state and three times Democratic candidate for the presidency, suffered public humiliation at the hands of Clarence Darrow, the ACLU lawyer. Cleverly drawing on literalistic interpretations of the Bible approved of by conservatives, Darrow showed that Bryan's knowledge of scripture and fundamentalist principles of interpretation was fatally flawed. Afflicted with diabetes, Bryan died shortly after the trial, a broken man. In the media treatment sight was lost of the moral issues that had been his primary concern. As a Democrat and populist, Bryan believed that German militarism, the ultimate cause of the First World War, had been a by-product of Darwin's theory of natural selection combined with Friedrich Nietzsche's ideas about the human Will to Power. Given the way in which ideas of Social Darwinism were subsequently put to use by the Nazis, he deserves more credit than he has been given. Shortly before the Second World War, Adolf Hitler would state in one of his speeches: '[Anyone] who has pondered on the order of this world realizes that its meaning lies in the warlike survival of the fittest.'

Anti-evolution laws remained on the statue books of several American states, and indeed were extended in some cases. But for the American public at large, fundamentalists were exposed as rural ignoramuses, rural hillbillies out of touch with modern thought. One of the major cultural events of 20th-century America, the Monkey Trial precipitated what might be called the 'withdrawal phase' of American fundamentalism – a retreat into the enclaves of churches and private educational institutions, such as Bob Jones University in South Carolina. In the mainstream academies, seminaries, and denominations, liberal theology, which accepted evolution as God's way of doing things, swept the board.

As Susan Harding explains, the regime of public religiosity that prevailed in America during the mid-20th century was secular in the limited sense, at least, that at the national-level signs of religious partisanship were voluntarily suppressed – though it remained for the most part incomplete, fragile, and, at times and places, seriously contested. The triumph of liberalism in the mainstream churches was at first tacitly endorsed by the fundamentalists who, for the most part, opted for the strategy of separation from the world. Logically, premillennialists should not care if the world goes from bad to worse, though they are charitably enjoined to rescue as many souls as they can. According to the Book of Revelation, the reign of the Antichrist preceding the Second Coming will be accompanied by all sorts of portents and signs of evil. As the saved remnant of humanity, true Christians (that is, fundamentalists) should even welcome these signs as proof that salvation is imminent. 'The darker the night gets, the lighter my heart gets', wrote Reuben Torrey, one of the editors of *The Fundamentals*.

Fundamentalists therefore saw the contempt to which they were exposed in the popular media after the Scopes trial as confirmation of their beliefs. The trend towards withdrawal did not mean, however, that American fundamentalism remained static. Despite its exclusion from the mainstream, the half-century from 1930 to 1980 saw a steady institutional growth, with numerous (mainly Baptist) churches seceding from national denominations in order to create an impressive national infrastructure of pastoral networks, parachurch organizations and superchurches, schools and colleges, book and magazine publishing industries, radio, television and direct-mail operations that built on older institutions created during the 19th-century revivals, such as the famous Moody Bible Institute in Chicago. Whilst mainstream America, abetted by an increasingly centralized media, remained unaware of what Jerry Falwell would call the 'sleeping giant' in its midst, the giant itself became progressively alarmed and annoyed at the encroachments of permissiveness and the growing assertiveness of mainstream secular culture.

The United States Constitution in its First Amendment disestablishes religion and creates what would become known, in Thomas Jefferson's famous phrase, as 'a wall of separation' between church and state. Whatever their political ambitions, American fundamentalists are constrained by this wall, which, for historical reasons, they are more likely than not to accept. As refugees from what they conceived to be the religious tyrannies of the Old World, the Protestant colonists who founded the United States in 1776 and won its independence from Britain were opposed to any alliance between state power and religious authority. Churches should be self-governing, autonomous institutions free from taxation and government interference. Nevertheless, since all of the Founding Fathers were Protestants, modern fundamentalists can plausibly argue that the United States was founded as a Christian – specifically, Protestant – nation. For them, the wall of separation does not mean that the state is atheist or even secular in the fullest sense of the word: merely that it maintains a posture of neutrality towards the different churches or denominations. However, with waves of Catholic migrants from Ireland arriving from the 1830s and Jewish immigration from Eastern and Central Europe from the latter part of the 19th century, denominational pluralism was extended far beyond what many people would have imagined during the 1780s (though not Thomas Jefferson, who believed in religious freedom for 'the infidel of every denomination').

A landmark Supreme Court decision in 1961 extended to secular humanists (non-believers) the legal protection accorded to followers of religious faiths. Ironically, this is the decision which fundamentalists now use in order to argue that secular humanism qualifies as a religion, for example when values associated with it appear in school curricula. They argue mischievously that it should be curbed by the state in order to maintain the 'wall of separation'. American fundamentalists are therefore constrained by the pluralistic religious culture in which they must operate. Rather than forming a religious party aimed at taking over the government, they lobby for power and influence within the Republican Party. Legislative successes at state level have included the reinstitution of daily prayers in some public schools, equal time rules for the teaching of evolution and creationism, or 'intelligent design' (a thinly disguised version of creationism that appears to be more scientific), and the overturning by a dozen or more states of the 1973 Supreme Court *Roe* v. *Wade* judgment repealing state bans on abortion. At the local level, fundamentalists have lobbied for the banning of books deemed irreligious from public school libraries or curricula. The banned titles have included such classics as Nathaniel Hawthorne's *The Scarlet Letter*, William Golding's *Lord of the Flies*, and books by Mark Twain, Joseph Conrad, and John Steinbeck, all of which have been seen as promoting the 'religion' of secular humanism by questioning faith in God or portraying religion negatively. These successes, however, have often been reversed by the courts after actions by organizations such as the ACLU and PAW (People for the American Way), a liberal lobby group. At the national level, fundamentalism is further constrained by the need to find conservative partners from beyond the ranks of Protestants.

On single issues such as abortion or the proposed amendment to the US Constitution granting Equal Rights for women (ERA), and the teaching of creationism or 'intelligent design' in schools, fundamentalist lobbying can be efficacious. (ERA failed after 'Christian' women were bused in their thousands to Washington.) In the wider political domain, however, American fundamentalists are faced with a dilemma. To collaborate with other conservative groups they must suppress or even abandon some of their theological objections to those – such as Mormons, Jews, or Catholics – whose religions they regard as being false.

The world of Islam presents a somewhat different perspective. The earliest reference to 'fundamentalism' in English I have found in relation to Islam is in a letter written in May 1937 by Sir Reader Bullard, British Minister in Jeddah, who stated that King Abd al-Aziz Ibn Saud has been 'coming out strong as a fundamentalist' by condemning women who mix with men under the cloak of progress. Bruce Lawrence suggests that the term 'Islamic fundamentalism' was coined by H. A. R. Gibb, the well known orientalist, in his book *Mohammedanism* (later retitled *Islam*), with reference to Jamal al-Din al-Afghani, the pan-Islamic reformer and political activist. Both the movements headed by Ibn Saud and Afghani could be said to have exhibited some of Wittgenstein's family resemblances: both involved a radical, in some cases an armed, defence of a religious tradition that felt itself to be challenged or threatened by modernity. But in both cases, the modernity in question was complicated by international politics. Ibn Saud's warriors, following in the tradition of Ibn Hanbal, Ibn Taymiyya, and Muhammad Ibn Abd al-Wahhab, the 18th-century

3. An anti-abortion demonstration outside the US Supreme Court

Arabian reformer, were certainly fundamentalists in the way they sought to return to the 7th-century scriptural roots of Islam, unsupplemented by the accumulated customs, doctrines, and traditions of subsequent centuries. Afghani, a masterful conspirator, polemicist, and political activist, can similarly be seen as fundamentalist in his desire to return to Islam's pristine roots, and in the efforts he made throughout his life to galvanize the Muslim rulers of his day into combating British imperialism. But far from unequivocally opposing the Enlightenment (one of the family traits ascribed to most fundamentalist movements), Afghani's attitude to modernity was thoroughly ambiguous. Hating imperialism, he nevertheless acknowledged the need for wholescale reforms of the Muslim religion, which he saw as decadent, decayed, and corrupt. His spirit is much closer to that of Martin Luther than to, say, a contemporary scriptural literalist such as Jerry Falwell.

The problems of definition are compounded when so-called Jewish fundamentalism is taken into account. As with Arabic, there is no indigenous Hebrew word that corresponds to 'fundamentalism'. The term usually employed for Jewish extremists by the Israeli media is *yamina dati*, the 'religious right'. Far from rejecting modernity, fundamentalists of the religious right such as Gush Emunim (the Bloc of the Faithful), are religious innovators. Whereas some traditionalist or orthodox groups known as the Haredim regarded the establishment of Israel as an impious pre-empting of the Messiah's role, Gush Emunim and other right-wing religious Zionists see the secular state as a stage towards Redemption. If Jewish fundamentalism can embrace such divergent alternatives, can the term be meaningful or useful?

The question, of course, is theoretical. By now it should be clear that the meanings, or possible applications, of the F-word have strayed far beyond the umbrella of the Abrahamic monotheisms (Judaism, Christianity, and Islam). For example, Sikh 'fundamentalists' took control of the Golden Temple of Amritsar in the Punjab, and when Indira Gandhi sent the troops in, they murdered her in revenge.

Hindu 'fundamentalists' demolished the Babri Masjid Mosque at Ayodhya, south-east of Delhi, in 1992, believing it to be the birthplace of the deity Rama (Lord Ram), setting off communal rioting that cost many thousands of lives (see Chapter 6). Buddhist monks in Sri Lanka have taken up arms against Tamil separatists, breaking with centuries of pacifism. For their part, the mostly secular Tamils, who developed the tactic of suicide bombing a decade before the Palestinians, sometimes require their vanguard squads to take an oath to the Hindu god Shiva.

'Fundamentalism' now encompasses many types of activity, not all of them religious. Critics of the World Bank and International Monetary Fund (IMF) such as George Soros, the financier, and Joseph Stiglitz, the Nobel Laureate, have accused the doctrinaire policies of 'market fundamentalism' dominant in Washington, for making global capitalism 'unsound and unsustainable' by forcing deregulation and tight fiscal restraints on the economies of developing nations, with dire consequences for the poorest sections of society. The wing of the Scottish National Party least disposed to cooperate with other parties in the Scottish Parliament has been described as fundamentalist by its opponents. In Germany, members of the Green Party who supported Joschka Fischer in joining former Chancellor Gerhard Schroeder's Red-Green coalition were described as *realos* (realists), in contrast to the *fundis* (fundamentalists) who held true to the Party's ideology of pacifism, opposition to nuclear power, and radical environmentalism. The tension between the two wings was brought to breaking point when Fischer, as Germany's foreign minister, supported the NATO bombing of Serbia in 1999 while his Green Party colleague, environment minister Jürgen Trittin, was pressured into abandoning a scheme to make car manufacturers pay for the cost of recycling old vehicles and forced to make painful compromises in his plans for phasing out nuclear power.

Similar tensions between ideological purists who stick to the fundamentals of their cause without compromising their principles, and the realists who argue that real gains can be achieved through bargaining and compromise, exist in all political and cultural movements; indeed, they are the very stuff of democratic politics – the energy of political life is most often released when the ideals of party activists are pitted against the realities of power. Virtually every movement, from animal rights to feminism, will embrace a spectrum ranging from uncompromising radicalism or extremism to pragmatic accommodationism. For feminist ultras such as Andrea Dworkin, virtually all penetrative sex is deemed to be rape. For some animal liberationists, every abattoir, however humane its procedures, is an extermination camp, while in the rhetoric of radical pro-lifers such as Pat Robertson, the 43 million foetuses 'murdered' since *Roe* v. *Wade* are an abomination comparable to the Nazi Holocaust.

At the borders of the semantic field it now occupies, the word 'fundamentalism' strays into extremism, sectarianism, doctrinairism, ideological purism. It seems doubtful, however, if these non-religious uses of the word are analytically useful. There may be some similarities in political and social psychology between, say, anti-abortionists, animal rightists, Green Party activists, Islamist agitators, and the Six Day Creationists (now modulated into 'intelligent designers') who sit on school boards in Kansas or southern California. A reluctance to compromise with one's deeply held principles is an obvious common trait. Such usages, however, seem to me to stray beyond Wittgenstein's family resemblances into something closer to mere analogy. Similarity does not necessarily imply kinship. The genetic bond that defines fundamentalism in its more central, and useful, meaning – the fundamentalist DNA, as it were – is sharper and more distinctive than extremism. The original Protestant use of the word anchors it in the responses of individual or collective selfhoods, of personal and group identities, to the scandal or shock of the Other.

Although many religious activists (especially the evangelical movements within Christianity and Islam) believe they have a universal mission to transform or convert the world, all religious traditions must face the *problématique* of their parochial origins, the embarrassing fact that saviours and prophets uttered divine words in specific languages to relatively small groups of people in certain localities at particular moments in time. The late John Lennon was correct in stating that the Beatles were more famous in their time than Jesus was in his. The original social context of the Bible, or the Koran, can never be recovered: modern Christians will never be Galilean peasants; Muhammad's Arab Bedouin have all but disappeared. Religious pluralism is an inescapable feature of modernity. It implies choice, inviting the suspicion that there may be more than one path to salvation (perhaps even a non-religious path). The surge of fundamentalist movements, or movements of religious revitalization, we are witnessing in many parts of the world is a response to globalization and, more specifically, to the crises for believers that inevitably follows the recognition that there are ways of living and believing other than those deemed to have been decreed by one's own tradition's version of the deity.

Chapter 2
The scandal of difference

The Egyptian historian Abd al-Rahman al-Jabarti (1754–1822)
wrote an account of Napoleon's invasion of Egypt in 1798 which
perfectly expresses the disdain as well as the fear experienced when
a traditional society is exposed to the brutal and outlandish
manners of outsiders. Al-Jabarti was no reactionary bigot. He
visited the Institut d'Egypte, and the outcome, the massive
23-volume *Description de l'Egypte*, is a monument to the science
of the Enlightenment. He was impressed by the dedication and
scholarship of the savants whom Napoleon had brought with his
train. He admitted, after observing experiments conducted by
French scientists, that 'these are things that the minds of people like
us cannot grasp'. But their religion, or lack of it, appalled him. In his
mind, French irreligion was assimilated to that of the *zindiqs*
(Manichaeans) and other enemies of Islam in its earliest phases.

A similar mood, intensified by bitterness at Western support for
Israel and the suppression of the Muslim Brotherhood by the
Egyptian dictator Gamal Abdul Nasser, pervades the writings of the
Islamist ideologue Sayyid Qutb. Imprisoned and tortured by
Nasser's police and executed in 1966 on what were almost certainly
trumped-up charges, Qutb concluded that Muslim society in the
Arab world and beyond had ceased to be Islamic, having relapsed to
the condition of *jahiliyya*, the paganism of the period of ignorance
that preceded the revelation of Islam. Just as God had authorized

> The French follow this rule: great and small, high and low, male and female are all equal. Sometimes they break this rule according to their whims and inclinations or reasoning. Their women do not veil themselves and have no modesty; they do not care whether they uncover their private parts. Whenever a Frenchman has to perform an act of nature he does so wherever he happens to be, even in full view of people, and he goes away as he is, without washing his private parts . . .
>
> (Abd al-Rahman al-Jabarti, *Napoleon in Egypt*)

Muhammad to fight the Meccan pagans before they eventually submitted to Islam, so Qutb in his prison writings provided the rationale that would later be used to justify the assassination of President Anwar Sadat in October 1981, as well as the Islamist attacks on the Egyptian and other nominally Muslim governments, on Western personnel and tourists, and the atrocity that killed nearly 3,000 people in New York and Washington on 11 September 2001. Though Qutb himself never explicitly advocated violence against individuals, the myth of the *jahiliyya* state, supported by the West, sustains Islamist militants from Algeria to the Philippines.

More than a century and a half separates al-Jabarti's chronicle and the prison writings of Sayyid Qutb. Jabarti was a scholar at the University of al-Azhar trained in the traditional Islamic sciences: the manners and customs of the French disturbed him in the same way that the Taliban, religious students raised in the rural madrasas (seminaries) of northern Pakistan and southern Afghanistan, were shocked by the appearance of unveiled women in the streets of Kabul when they took over the city in 1996. Qutb, however, was a member of the Egyptian intellectual elite. A protégé of the writer Taha Hussein and the poet Abbas Mahmud al-Aqqad, leading lights

> Humanity today is living in a large brothel! One has only to glance at its press, films, fashion shows, beauty contests, ballrooms, wine bars, and broadcasting stations! Or observe its mad lust for naked flesh, provocative postures, and sick, suggestive statements in literature, the arts and the mass media! And add to all this the system of usury which fuels man's voracity for money and engenders vile methods for its accumulation and investment, in addition to fraud, trickery, and blackmail dressed up in the garb of law.
>
> (Sayyid Qutb)

in Egypt's liberal Western-oriented intelligentsia, he received government funding to study in America, where he attended universities in Washington DC, Colorado, and California. It was exposure to Western (particularly American) culture, not ignorance, that led to his revulsion. His is the paradigmatic case of the born-again Muslim who, having adopted or absorbed many modern or foreign influences, discards them in his search for personal identity and cultural authenticity. The term 'fundamentalist' may seem appropriate, but in Qutb's case it is still problematic. Far from espousing received theological certainties or defending Muslim society against foreign encroachments, Qutb's understanding of Islam was almost Kierkegaardian in its individualism: his authentic Muslim was one who espouses a very modern kind of revolution against 'the deification of man', against injustice, and against political, economic, racial, and religious prejudice.

Behind both these responses, Jabarti's and Qutb's, lies a particularly Islamic response to the loss of cultural hegemony. Islam, whose formative institutions were created during a period of historic triumph, may be described as being 'programmed for victory' or 'hard-wired for success'. Outside the Shia minority tradition which, like Christianity, has myths and theologies for dealing with failure, Islam has been a triumphalist faith. Non-Muslims were tolerated on condition that they accepted their subordinate status. Jabarti's perplexity and Qutb's rage are both responses to the scandalous fact that the Enlightenment, with all the consequences it held for human progress, occurred not in the Muslim world, whose scientific and humanistic culture prepared the ground for it, but in the West, a barbarous and, to Muslim minds, backward region whose primitive Christian faith had been superseded by Islam, God's final revelation.

The crisis that normative Islam faces in its relation with the contemporary world is partly historical. It flows from the contradiction between the collective memory of the triumphal progress of Islam under Muhammad and his immediate successors and the experience of recent political failure during the colonial and post-colonial periods, when most of the Islamic world came under Western political, cultural, and commercial domination. Outside the Arabian peninsular, most of the world that had lived and prospered for centuries under the imperial faith of Islam became subject to European imperialism in some form, prompting reformers such as Sayyid Ahmed Khan in India and Muhammad Abduh in Egypt to ally themselves to European power in order to try to accommodate the scientific and humanistic knowledge of the West within the cultural norms of Islam. The result was a *de facto* separation of religious and secular culture contrary to the stated nostrums of Islamic tradition, which denied any formal distinction between religion and the world (Arabic, *din wa dunya*). Modernization (including political modernization) proceeded along the secular path, whilst religion remained for the most part in the custody of traditionalist *ulama* who (unlike their counterparts in Protestant seminaries) avoided the challenge of modernizing the religion from within.

The fundamentalist impulse in Islam thus takes a different form from its counterpart in Protestant Christianity, where the struggle between fundamentalism and liberalism was for the most part waged inside the churches and the teaching institutions that served them. In the majority Sunni tradition it is driven mainly by the secular elites, beneficiaries of modern scientific and technical educations, who wish to reintegrate the religious, cultural, and political life of their societies along Islamic lines: the shorthand for this aspiration is the 'restoration of the Sharia' (Islamic law). Scholars make a distinction between those Islamists who put more emphasis on voluntary Islamization from below, through preaching, the building or taking over of state mosques, the creation of charitable and social welfare networks, and cultural activities including women's *halaqas* (circles) or discussion groups; and Islamization from above, involving the exercise of influence at state level, including the take over, by revolutionary or military means, of state power. The family resemblance to Protestant fundamentalism may seem tenuous: but there is an underlying similarity. This is the holistic, even totalitarian, idea of a political order governed by God.

Underlying both these visions lies a myth of the golden age when the norms of the tradition are presumed to have held sway. Many of the fundamentalist groups investigated by scholars subscribe to this mythical idea of a time when the problems and conflicts that beset modern society (such as drug and alcohol abuse, unregulated sexuality, criminal behaviour, and child abuse) were deemed to be much less prevalent than they are today. Muslim fundamentalists tend to trace this golden age to the era of the Prophet Muhammad and his immediate successors, the Rightly Guided Caliphs, though in the collective imagination this era of innocence and tranquillity is also predicated on pre-colonial times. American fundamentalists tend to idealize the 1950s, just after the American victory in the Second World War, before the disillusionment occasioned by the Vietnam War and the youth rebellion of the 1960s (along with sex, drugs, and rock and roll) set in. But like the Islamists, they also look back to the time of origins, in this case to the American Revolution, whose founding fathers are deemed to have been God-fearing Christians. Hindu and Jewish fundamentalists also subscribe to myths of a golden age. Hindus venerate the Kingdom of Ayodhya, whose ruler Lord Rama they wish to restore to his temple on the site of the Babri Masjid, the mosque built by Babur, the first Moghul conqueror, which militants demolished in 1992. Some Jewish fundamentalists hark back to the era of David, and to Solomon, builder of the First Temple in Jerusalem. Its restoration, like that of Ayodhya, would necessitate the destruction of two Muslim shrines, the Dome of the Rock and the al-Aqsa mosque, from where Muhammad is supposed to have ascended to heaven. Others, such as the Haredim and members of Hasidic orders look back to a more recent era. Wearing the frock coats, broad-brimmed hats, and ringlets of the 18th-century *shtetels* of Eastern Europe, they seek to preserve the close-knit, Halakha-governed, autonomous communities prior to the Jewish Enlightenment, before the processes of modernization and secularization began. Orthodox Jewish groups which strictly observe the Halakha had been conditioned by a fundamentalist refusal to abandon the condition of exile long before anti-Semitic persecutions drove them back into the ghettos of Eastern Europe. Transplanted to Palestine after the Holocaust by necessity rather than choice, their attitudes towards the secular Zionist state range from formal non-recognition to *de facto* collaboration.

Most of the Haredim accept that it is pointless to try to impose the Halakha on the rest of society: the state of the Jews can become a Jewish state only when the Messiah comes. The attitude corresponds to that of the premillennial Protestants, who see themselves as the saved remnant of humanity pending the Return of Jesus. Since the condition of exile is an existential one, an alienation from the godhead which cannot be overcome by human action, some of the Haredim do not even recognize Israel as the Jewish homeland, although, pragmatically, they have made their accommodations with it. Instead, they reconfigure themselves as the real Jews, now in exile within the secular Zionist state. Gush Emunim, by contrast, are future-oriented: like some radical Islamists and postmillennial Protestants, they seek to establish utopian society based on the rule of God.

> The encounter of the world faiths is still only just beginning, even today. There are many historical and sociological reasons for the delay. Chief among them, no doubt, is the understandable belief that one's own tradition, after long centuries of development and diversification, contains within itself resources varied enough to meet the needs of all types of individual. This argument for staying within one's own camp is, however, vulnerable to something that we might call religion-shock on the analogy of culture-shock. Religion-shock occurs when someone who is a strong and sincere believer in his own faith confronts, without evasion and without being able to explain it away, the reality of an entirely different form of faith, and faces the consequent challenge to his own deepest assumptions.
>
> (Don Cupitt, *The Sea of Faith*)

In all such cases the vision is monocultural. The group or enclave it supports rejects the pluralism and diversity which constitute one the defining characteristics of the modern world. Modernity pluralizes, introducing choices (including religious choices) where none existed before. Before modern forms of travel and communications made people living in different cultural systems aware of each other, most people assumed that their own way of life or system of beliefs were the norm. The same considerations applied to social life and most types of industrial activity. Everywhere, modernity entails diversification and specialization as well as innovation.

For pre-modern Judaism, the barriers created by religious identity and external hostility were mutually reinforcing. Similarly, pre-modern Catholic Christianity enforced strict religious conformity, and it was only after centuries of conflict between

Catholics and Protestants (and within Protestantism) – conflicts that assisted the emergence of the Enlightenment – that a *modus vivendi* between the two faiths was achieved.

Compared to pre-Enlightenment Christendom, the record of Islam is impressive. Pre-modern Islam formally tolerated Jews and Christians as *dhimmis*, or peoples of the book entitled to Muslim protection, a status later extended to Zoroastrians, Hindus, and adherents of other scriptural religions. Protection, however, is not the same as full religious tolerance. The *dhimmis* were not accorded legal equality and in most Islamic societies rules affecting marriage, legal testimony, house construction, costume, and animal transport pointedly emphasized their inferior social status. Islamists in Egypt, Pakistan, and Bangladesh (among other countries) have demanded the restoration of *dhimmi* status to non-Muslims (including Coptic Christians and Hindus), as well as to Muslim groups they consider heretical, which would limit their rights as citizens.

Though fundamentalists, as we shall see, have not been slow to embrace such aspects of modernity as they find congenial, especially modern technologies (including radio, television, electronics, and armaments) they consider helpful to their cause, they do not or cannot fully accept religious pluralism. Islamist extremists in Upper Egypt have tried to extract the *jizya* tax from the Christian Coptic minority, a payment that would symbolize their inferior status. The Hindu fundamentalists of the BJP (Bharatiya Janata Party) and RSS (Rashtriya Svayamsevak Sangh, or 'national union of volunteers') believe that Indian nationhood must be based on caste, the social categories recognized in classical Hinduism, thus excluding Muslims, Sikhs, Christians, tribal peoples, and even non-resident Indians (NRIs) from their notion of Indian identity. Jewish fundamentalists tend to be narrower in their definitions of what constitutes Jewish identity than secular Zionists. The extremists among them, such as Baruch Goldstein, who killed some 30 Arab worshippers at the Tomb of the Patriarchs in Hebron in 1994, and his mentor, Rabbi Meir Kahane, held views about

Arabs that were remarkably similar to Adolf Hitler's views about the Jews. Premillennial Protestants believe that following the imminent return of Christ those who accept the Messiah (that is, born-again Christians, and 144,000 righteous Jews) will be raptured into Heaven, while the unrighteous majority (including nominal Christians and unsaved members of other religious traditions) will perish miserably. Indeed, for many conservative Protestants, Catholics are not Christians, Episcopalians and Unitarians are atheists, Mormonism is a dangerous cult, while Hinduism, Buddhism, and other non-Western religions are Satanic. As for Islam, Jerry Falwell spoke for many American evangelicals after 9/11 by describing Muhammad as a terrorist.

In practice, some tactical accommodations with pluralism may be necessary, and fundamentalists who want to pursue a political agenda (such as banning abortion or blocking the constitutional amendment guaranteeing equal rights for women) have found it expedient to collaborate with religious groups they regard as heretical. In principle, however, the commands of God as understood by the faithful are non-negotiable, absolute, and unconditional. For Jerry Falwell, all who fail after hearing it to accept the Christian gospel are doomed. In the Islamist view, the same goes for the Koran and teachings of Muhammad.

Since God is reported to have said different things to the numerous individuals claiming to speak on his behalf, belief in the truth held by one tradition necessarily excludes all others. This is especially so in the Abrahamic tradition of Western monotheism, where confessions are deemed to be exclusive: in the mainstream, orthodox versions of these faiths one cannot be a Muslim and a Christian, or a Christian and a Jew. In a globalized culture where religions are in daily contact with their competitors, denial of pluralism is a recipe for conflict.

Yet acceptance of pluralism relativizes truth. Once it is allowed that there are different paths to truth, a person's religious allegiance

> The Quran does not claim that Islam is the true compendium of rites and rituals, and metaphysical beliefs and concepts, or that it is the proper form of religious (as the word religion is nowadays understood in Western terminology) attitude of thought and action for the individual. Nor does it say that Islam is the true way of life for the people of Arabia, or for the people of any particular country or for the people preceding any particular age (say, the Industrial Revolution), No! Very explicitly, for the entire human race, there is only one way of life which is Right in the eyes of God and that is al-Islam.
>
> (Sayyid Abu Ala Mawdudi, *The Religion of Truth*)

becomes a matter of choice, and choice is the enemy of absolutism. Fundamentalism is one response to the crisis of faith brought about by awareness of differences. As Clifford Geertz once put it:

> From now on no one will leave anyone else alone. When traditional cultures no longer feel left alone or when they want to intrude on the other of whom they become aware, tradition ceases to be tradition in the traditional sense of the word.

Religious pluralism, by which I mean the policy of granting public recognition to more than one religious tradition, is as integral to modernity as cars, aeroplanes, television, and the internet: indeed, it is a consequence of a world where everyone is increasingly aware of everyone else, where 'no one leaves anyone else alone'. Since the Reformation broke the religious monopoly of the Roman Catholic Church in the West, pluralism has been institutionalized, and although the process was a gradual one (with Catholics in Britain, for example, only granted the vote in the 19th century), the spread of pluralism has become unstoppable. The wars of religion in Germany, culminating in the Peace of Westphalia (1648), established pluralism under the principle *cuius regio, eius religio* – 'religion belongs to the ruler'. This was not yet toleration: rulers retained the right to impose their religion on their subjects, with Catholics persecuted in Protestant domains, and vice versa. But it marked an irrevocable step in its direction. Boundaries being porous, states acquired minorities. Though religious conformity was rigorously enforced in countries such as France, England, and Spain, uniformity proved unattainable. Toleration was the political consequence of the Reformation's challenge to the Church's monopoly. In due course it became a prerequisite of Enlightenment thought, 'an apanage of reason', as Voltaire would call it. Superstition and dogma, originally the targets of Protestants, became the bugbears of all Enlightenment thinkers. For Pierre Bayle, writing in the 1690s, God was too benevolent a being to be the author of anything so pernicious as the revealed religions, which 'carry in themselves the inexterminable seeds of war, slaughter and injustice'. By the mid-18th century the deists had assimilated God to pure reason, decoupling the deity from the religions that claimed to speak on His behalf.

Protestant America, founded by religious refugees from Europe, developed its own distinctive style of pluralism known as denominationalism, becoming after the Revolution the first polity in the world with an explicit guarantee of religious freedom. (The French and Russian revolutions, by contrast, were violently anti-religious in their initial phases.) Jefferson's 'wall of separation' between church and state was intended to prevent any one tradition or denomination from exercising state power over the others. American churches are privileged self-governing enclaves. They are self-financing, though as non-profit corporations they benefit from negative subsidies since their earnings are free from tax (though there are grey areas such as rents and property where their tax-exempt status is hotly contested by government). In practice, the divine supermarket brought into being by religious deregulation enabled the free churches such as Baptists and Methodists (minorities in Europe) to expand more rapidly than the more tightly ordered churches such as the Anglicans, Congregationalists, or Presbyterians. The latter had enjoyed state patronage during the colonial period, with each of the Thirteen Colonies having its own establishment: Massachusetts was Congregationalist, New York Presbyterian, Maryland Catholic, Virginia Anglican, and so forth. As Will Herberg observed half a century ago, the denomination is a uniquely American creation. It is 'the non-conformist sect become central and normative'. It differs from the European idea of the Church 'in that it would never claim to be the national institution', but it also differs from the sect in being 'socially established, thoroughly institutionalised and nuclear to the society in which it is found'. In American Christendom, the fringe becomes the centre. Even the Roman Catholic Church became subject to the democratizing effects of denominationalism, as the Frenchman Alexis de Tocqueville noted on his famous visit to the United States in 1825.

In Europe religious toleration and the secularization of government occurred more gradually, with historic state churches retaining a degree of institutional monopoly. In Germany and Scandinavia, churches are subsidized out of taxation; in Britain, the established churches (Anglican in England and Wales, Presbyterian in Scotland) are the beneficiaries of endowments built up over centuries. The Catholic Church in France, Italy, and Spain is formally separate from the state (with religion in France limited, since 1905, to the private sphere), but it nevertheless retains a powerful institutional presence through its educational establishments and the symbolism of its architecture. Paradoxically, the closer connections between church and state in Europe seem to have facilitated the secularization of society, with regular church attendance (as distinct from formal church membership) in rapid decline in most European countries. In the United States, by contrast, deregulation and the ensuing competition between churches, the absence of an anti-clerical tradition, and the cultural presence of Protestantism as a civil religion have combined to make Christianity, the religion of 86% of the population, an important element in public life, despite (or perhaps because of) disestablishment. In contrast to Europe, where many of the educational, pastoral, and social functions once performed by the church have been taken over by state authorities, America's churches still dispose of significant social power. Under certain conditions that power becomes political.

At the same time, conservative Christians (including some Catholics and Mormons), as well as some Jews, have felt themselves to be increasingly under attack as the state has encroached upon areas previously considered to be the preserve of religious communities. Throughout the United States, and not just in the Bible Belt of Texas and the Old South, fundamentalists have taken action in defence of their idea of a Christian America. Successive court decisions, usually backed by mainstream liberal denominations, have outlawed racial segregation and discrimination against women, racial minorities, and homosexuals. Prayer has been banned in publicly funded schools in furtherance of church–state separation, and non-Christians of all persuasions, including outright atheists and secular humanists, have been accorded the legal protections the Constitution guarantees. When these and many other developments threatened what they saw as their freedom, fundamentalists were moved to fight back. In their view, the pluralism permitted under the Constitution was implicitly limited to Protestant Christianity; and while it might be stretched to include Jews and Catholics, the idea that 'Satanic Hindus', 'terrorist Muslims', or outright atheists could benefit from laws intended to preserve denominational pluralism within the Judaeo-Christian fold was anathema.

To the scandal of difference one should add the scandal of social and behavioural change. As Steve Bruce explains in the American context,

> one need not follow fundamentalists in their uncritical attitude to
> the past, their blanket condemnation of the present, nor in their

explanation of the ways in which the world has changed to accept that divorce is now common, as is drug addiction, that homosexuality is accepted in many circles as an alternative lifestyle, that housewife is a devalued status, that the separation of church and state (once interpreted as denominational neutrality) is now taken to imply secularity, and so on.

He concludes that the changes that have been promoted and welcomed by atheists, feminists, racial minorities, and liberals have fundamentally altered the moral, social, and political culture of America and moved it away from the standards and practices that fundamentalists regard as biblical.

From their own perspective, Christian fundamentalists may have a point. State legislation, for example in education, has become increasingly intrusive. First public schools were desegregated, with bussing introduced to assist racial integration. When conservatives responded by establishing their own independent Christian schools, the state intervened by removing their tax-exempt status if they appeared segregationist. It supported state legislatures which required the licensing even of independent schools. In the media, religious conservatives of all persuasions experienced the intrusion of secular humanism or Godless values in such areas as the public acceptance of nudity, homosexuality, sex outside marriage, and the termination of pregnancies.

In other countries also, the reactions generated by similar changes can be seen as a response to the increasing intrusiveness on the part of the state. In traditional Islamic societies before the colonial intervention in the 19th century, the state had a watchdog role that allowed civil society to manage itself with a minimum of political interference. Formally the Islamic ruler, the Sultan or 'authority', was subject to Islamic law, although in practice his governance could be supplemented by royal decrees. Though the Sultan appointed the judges, the law was interpreted and administered by the *ulama*, a class of literate scholars often tied by family links to the merchant class. Though often thought of as harsh by modern standards because of the use of corporal punishments for certain categories of crime, the thrust of the law was not so much to uphold the state as to maintain social harmony by mediating between contending parties. Challenged by the rising power of the European nations, reforming autocrats used their prerogative powers to whittle away the autonomy of civil society in Muslim lands. Their modern successors, in most cases, have continued along the same path. In the postcolonial era the Muslim world has seen a progressive intrusion of the state into areas hitherto reserved for voluntary activity, including education, social welfare, industrial production, and even the sacred arena of family life. In the Arab world especially, nationalist regimes enthusiastically adopted the Marxist model imported from Eastern Europe. The single-party state, reinforced by oil monopolies, became the primary agency for political, economic, and social mobilization, ruling by the carrot of state patronage and stick of police repression.

Though the Jewish example differs significantly, similar patterns can still be observed. From its beginnings in 19th-century Europe, the Zionist movement which culminated in the creation of Israel in 1948 was dominated by secular intellectuals. Throughout most of the half-century of Israel's existence the prevailing tone has been secular and democratic. The religious parties represented in the Knesset (the Israeli parliament) have extracted concessions from successive governments on state funding for religious education, exemptions from military service for yeshiva (seminary) students, marriage and divorce, and other questions of personal status, including the problematic question of Jewish identity (the 'who is a Jew?' controversy). For a religious tradition forged during centuries of exile, however, a state in which Jews are a majority poses special problems. Far from permitting a relaxation of the Halakhic rules, customs formulated under the conditions of exile are adhered to as rigidly as they were in the diaspora.

One can discern in such paradoxes the inertia or inherent

conservatism underpinning group identities where continuity is sustained through repetition. Ulster Protestants re-enact and ritualize the events to which they believe they owe their religious liberty – the Battle of the Boyne on 12 July 1690, the closing of the Gates of Londonderry by the Apprentice Boys in August 1689. Muslim settlers in Surinam (formerly Dutch Guyana) brought in from Java in the 19th century still pray westwards towards Mecca, instead of facing east, as their new location should require. Fundamentalist movements may be grounded emotionally in communities forged under minority conditions, where the sense of embattlement, of being an island of virtue or faith in a sea of ignorance or sin, is strong. But unlike sects such as the Amish, who may be happy to be left alone in horse-drawn, zipper-free isolation, the fundamentalism with which we are primarily concerned has broader ambitions. Seldom content with defending its minority status against the onslaughts of a pluralistic, secular world, it strives to fight back by exercising power, directly or indirectly. The encroachments of modernity through state power and state bureaucracies are pervasive and continuous and a constant challenge to all religious traditions. For the activist fundamentalist (as distinct from the passive traditionalist), the quest for salvation cannot be realized by withdrawing into a cultural enclave.

Chapter 3
The snares of literalism

Words strain,
Crack and sometimes break, under the burden,
Under the tension, slip, slide, perish,
Decay with imprecision, will not stay in place,
Will not stay still.

(T. S. Eliot, 'Burnt Norton')

Fundamentalists everywhere tend towards a literalist interpretation
of the texts they revere. A survey by the Gallup organization in 1980
found that 40% of the American public claimed to believe that the
Bible is the actual word of God and is to be taken literally, word for
word. Similarly, most believing Muslims, not just those described as
Islamists or militants, are fundamentalist in the sense that they take
the Koran to be the literal Word of God, as dictated to the Prophet
Muhammad through the agency of the Angel Gabriel (Jibreel).
Since it was assembled by the Third Caliph Uthman (reigned 644–
656 CE) the text is considered perfect, complete, and unalterable.
For conservative Muslim scholars as for radical fundamentalists,
the style of historical criticism that sees the language of revelation
as a human construct, reflecting the knowledge and prejudice of its
time, is anathema. The Egyptian academic Nasr Abu Zaid, who
ventured to use modern literary critical methodology in his
approach to the Koran, was forced into exile. Higher criticism of the

Koran, where the text is deconstructed in accordance with methods developed by biblical scholars since the 18th century, is still very largely confined to scholars who are not Muslims. Examples include the work of John Wansbrough, Patricia Crone, and Gerald Hawting, Western scholars of Islam who do not accept the traditional view of its origins as related in the earliest texts.

There is more to literalism, however, than appears at first sight. A straightforward definition means reading the text at its plainest, most obvious. For some fundamentalists that would mean, for example, that when the Bible, in Genesis 1, tells us that God created the world in six days and rested on the seventh, the word 'day' corresponds to the usual dictionary definition of a 24-hour period (or perhaps a 12-hour period in which day is contrasted with night). Some fundamentalist theologians, however, retreat from this definition by arguing that since night and day as experienced by humans are caused by the earth turning on its axis, the days prior to the Creation can be understood to mean geological ages. In support of this, they cite a verse from Psalm 90: 'a thousand years in Thy sight are like yesterday', which shows that 'in other passages of scripture the word "day" is employed figuratively of a time of undefined length'. The issue, according to the liberal theologian James Barr, is not so much about literalism as *inerrancy*.

At its starkest, literalism means that the letter or exact wording of a text carries the whole weight of its meaning, excluding any unmentioned or extraneous data. An example is a well known case in British law. A wealthy Scot who lived in Edinburgh named in his will the National Society for the Prevention of Cruelty to Children (NSPCC) rather than the Scottish NSPCC, an entirely different charity – although he had shown some interest in the latter during his lifetime. Despite the arguments of the Scottish charity's lawyers that the NSPCC, based in London, was unknown to the benefactor, the Law Lords awarded the legacy to the London society on the ground that there was no explicit indication of the benefactor's intention to leave it to the Scottish society.

Sacred texts, however, rarely lend themselves to mechanical literalism in this way. Fundamentalists in general avoid addressing ambiguities of language by arguing that the plain meanings of scriptures are an integral part of their moralizing purpose. Thus the 19th-century Protestant theologian T. H. Horne insisted that,

> in common life, no prudent or conscientious person, who either commits his sentiments to writing or utters anything, intends that a diversity of meanings should be attached to what he writes or says; and consequently, neither his readers, nor those who hear him, affix to it any other than the true and obvious sense.

For fundamentalists the same is supposed to apply, *a fortiori*, to the writers of scripture inspired by the Holy Spirit (or, in the case of Islam, to the words of the Koran dictated to Muhammad by God or the agency of the angel).

Literalism, however, contains pitfalls of its own making. The understanding of texts in their literal sense as distinct from their mythical or allegorical meanings may open those very floodgates of textual criticism to which fundamentalists are most adamantly opposed. As Barr points out, the contradictions and anomalies in the Bible were spotted not by scholars primarily concerned with its mythological or allegorical meanings, but by literalists who paid close attention to the plain meanings of the text.

In the 11th century CE Isaac ibn Yashush, Jewish physician to one of the Muslim rulers in Spain, pointed out that the list of Edomite kings in Genesis 36 named several who lived long after Moses was supposed to have died. Thereafter early modern sceptics, including Thomas Hobbes and Baruch Spinoza, began to note details in the Pentateuch that seemed inconsistent with Mosaic authorship. From the 19th century, modern source criticism saw a consensus developing around the theme of multiple authorship. At present, there is hardly a biblical scholar in the world actively working on the problem who would claim that the Five Books of Moses were written by Moses, or by any one person. Similar findings apply to other Old Testament books. Textual criticism has revealed in the New Testament a mosaic or patchwork of materials from which the canon containing the Four Gospels, the Acts of the Apostles, the Epistles of Paul and Peter, and the Book of Revelation were constructed.

The *problématique* of literalist interpretation lies in the assumption that words can be understood separately from the hearer or reader's presuppositions about their context, meaning, or intent. 'Calling a spade a spade' is only meaningful when one is familiar with a certain type of garden tool – one that is now being superseded by small tractors and other power-driven machines. The original auditors of the scriptures or their earliest readers were people of their times. However hard fundamentalists try to resist the thrust of historical criticism, by insisting that God's Word is Timeless and Eternal, the facts alluded to in the scriptures can only be defended, as Barr points out, by shifting the ground away from literalism and towards inerrancy.

Thus Maurice Bucaille, in a book popular with Islamic fundamentalists, claims that the Koran contains references to many scientific facts of recent discovery, such as atoms, particles, and viruses. The perils of 'pure' literalism are illustrated by the famous example of Sheikh Abdullah bin Baz, the former chief mufti of Saudi Arabia, who on the basis of Koranic references to the 'seven heavens' of the Ptolemaic system, threatened to excommunicate anyone subscribing to the Copernican cosmology that replaced it in the 17th century. Embarrassed by the scandal occasioned by the worthy sheikh's views, which the Egyptian press took pleasure in publicizing, most Islamists now interpret the 'seven heavens' figuratively.

In one way the sheikh's *fatwa* is a benchmark in the transition from traditionalism to fundamentalism, the point where traditionalism becomes self-consciously reactive. Whereas the true traditionalist does not know he is a traditionalist, the fundamentalist is forced by the logic of his desire to defend tradition into making strategic selections. Textual anomalies are either denied, or subsumed into the hermeneutics of inerrancy, where the burden of proof is shifted from God to humanity. They can then be explained as errors of human understanding, rather than flaws in the text itself. Bin Baz's insistence *after* the Copernican revolution that the sun goes round the earth is quite different from the position of the pre-Copernican astronomers. He has in fact taken up an attitude to evidence which the pre-Copernicans had not been able to consider, and which would in all reasonable probability have caused them to modify their Ptolemaic views, if they had had access to it.

By a similar logic, the doctrine of inerrancy finesses the problem of literalism. An obvious example lies in the miracle stories that abound in the Old and New Testaments. Far from taking the medieval or traditionalist view of miracles, according to which God intervenes in natural processes by causing waters to rise up, or the sun to stand still, fundamentalist commentators tend to rationalize miracles by suggesting that they accord with natural processes such as earthquakes or landslides, or astronomical conjunctions. While not denying the possibility of miracles in principle, they tend to de-emphasize them in fact.

Some Islamic fundamentalist commentators also shy away from strict literalism in their interpretations of the Koran. Sayyid Qutb, the most influential of modern Sunni theorists in the Arab world, is best known for redefining the concept of *jahiliyya*, the age of ignorance before the coming of Islam, in terms of the modern state, thereby de-legitimizing it. Executed for his participation in an alleged plot to overthrow President Gamal Abdul Nasser in 1966, Qutb achieved a kind of posthumous revenge on the infidel government which martyred him: his resurrection of the writings of the 13th-century Hanbali scholar Ibn Taymiyya contributed indirectly to the murder of President Anwar Sadat in 1981. But while doubtless a militant, perhaps even an extremist, in his implacable hostility to the *jahiliyya* state, Qutb was hardly fundamentalist in the sense of taking a literalistic view of scripture. The 30-volume commentary on the Koran Qutb wrote in prison is full of a rationalist exegesis extolling the creative power of God in nature. His position is consistent with that of several modern Muslim writers who, like liberal Protestants, have accepted Darwinian evolution as 'God's way of doing things'. There are numerous passages in the Koran extolling Allah's creative power which Muslim scholars could cite as being consistent with evolutionary theory: for example in 22: 5 Allah tells Muhammad, 'We have created you [i.e. humanity] from dust, then from sperm, then from a little lump of flesh formed and unformed, that we may make it clear for you.' Following the example of Muhammad Abduh, Muslim writers tended to read modern scientific ideas into the Koran, while asserting that such concepts really had Islamic roots and that nothing in the divine text contradicted them.

'We can only seek God in His Word' wrote Jean Calvin, 'nor think of Him otherwise than according to the Word'. The cult of the text was always implicit in Protestantism, where biblical authority outweighed the cumulative tradition represented by the teaching and authority of the Catholic Church. Here an important question arises: can Catholics be fundamentalists? Given that the F-word originated with Protestant evangelicals protesting at the encroachments of liberal theology, does it apply to conservative Catholics who hold similar views?

The problem is complicated, however, by a defining feature of Catholicism that is in direct contrast to the cult of the text to be found in the Protestant and mainstream Islamic traditions: loyalty to the Church as an institution embodying a tradition of religious authority as important as scripture itself. The Catholic equivalent of fundamentalism is known as *intégrisme* in French, integralism in English. Until quite recently, the term *fondamentalisme* was not even found in French dictionaries to refer to a religious doctrine. Structurally, integralism is the equivalent of fundamentalism. It cares less, however, for a literalism of the book than for what one Jesuit scholar calls 'papal fundamentalism: a literal, ahistorical, and nonhermeneutical reading of papal pronouncements, even papal *obiter dicta*, as a bulwark against the tides of relativism, the claims of science, and the inroads of modernity'.

A family resemblance to integralism may be found in other religious traditions that emphasize the integrity, or divine quality, of religious leadership – for example, among Buddhist followers of the Dalai Lama, or Ismaili Shii followers of the Aga Khan, or some Ithnashari Shiis loyal to the late Ayatollah Khomeini. Loyalism directed towards an institution or person, however, even if carried to the point of fanaticism, stands in marked contrast to the forms that fundamentalism takes in the scripturally oriented versions of Judaism, Christianity, and Islam, where adherence to the text (or, rather, particular interpretations of the text) supersedes traditional forms of authority. This is especially the case in Arab Muslim societies such as Egypt and Algeria, where the Islamist movements are mostly led, not by members of the religious establishment represented by the traditionally educated rabbical class of *ulama*, but by religious autodidacts emerging from secondary schools and universities. The revolt of this newly enfranchised class of intellectuals, who usually come from rural backgrounds, has parallels with the Reformation in Europe, which coincided with the invention of printing and the extension of literacy into new social strata. Similarly, the original fundamentalists who waged 'battle royal' against the liberals within their own churches were in many cases rebels within their own institutions. Catholic integralists are constrained against rebelling by their loyalty to the leadership.

Inevitably, the strains are strongest when the leadership moves in a liberal direction. The reforms of Vatican II (1962–5) initiated by Pope John XXIII precipitated the secessionist movement under Monsignor Marcel Lefebvre in France and the 'Tradition, Property, Family' movement in Latin America. The reforms of Aga Khan III (1887–1957), a radical modernizer within the Ismaili Shii tradition, provoked a secession by some members of his community in East Africa, who joined or rejoined the larger Ithnashari Shii denomination. Buddhist communities in Tibet have suffered divisions because of the meddling of the Chinese authorities. However, in traditions where spiritual authority has been sanctioned by centuries of authoritarian leadership vested in a hereditary line of personages such as the Ismaili Imamate, or a charismatic office such as the papacy, secession is the exception.

Nevertheless there are some notable 'family resemblances'. The doctrine of papal infallibility adopted at Vatican I (1869–70) was a response to the same liberal or modernizing tendencies to which the original fundamentalists were responding during the first two decades of the 20th century, with papal infallibility corresponding to biblical inerrancy. In both cases, the fundamentalists/integralists took central orthodox symbols and highlighted or exaggerated them, enabling them to appeal to larger constituencies within their respective traditions. Both groups were caught up in a 'battle royal' against their more liberal co-religionists. Both sought to adopt elements of modernity on their own terms, seeking to be *in* modernity (and to influence its direction), but not *of* it.

Just as the Catholic Church only adopted the doctrine of papal infallibility when liberal theology was beginning to make itself felt, the doctrine of scriptural inerrancy only came to the fore among Protestants when traditional understandings of scripture began to be challenged.

As explained above, inerrancy is not the same as literalism, and may even produce opposite conclusions. Where literalist readings may logically lead to the deconstruction of texts, inerrancy when pursued systematically requires textual harmonization. Since the inerrant Bible as understood by fundamentalists is supposed to correspond to the historical actuality of real events in real time (as distinct from mythical events whose significance may be understood symbolically or spiritually), conservative commentators try to edit different versions of the same stories into a coherent narrative structure.

A well known example concerns the New Testament story of the cleansing of the Temple by Jesus, when he threw out the money-lenders. In the synoptic Gospels (Matthew, Mark, and Luke) the incident occurs at the very end of his ministry, at the beginning of Passion week (the week of the Crucifixion); whereas John has it at the very beginning of his ministry. Liberal theologians may explain the discrepancy by showing how John uses the episode to illustrate the Gnostic theme of the 'Word made Flesh' that resonates throughout the fourth Gospel. The conservative commentator Graham Swift provides a much simpler explanation: Jesus cleansed the Temple twice. The same methodology produces two ascensions of Jesus into heaven, since Luke has this occur on the same day as the resurrection whilst Acts makes it happen 40 days later, after Jesus had appeared to the disciples. Multiple ascensions, like dual Temple cleansings, allow both narratives to be taken literally, as real events that happened in real time, 'out there' in the world. To be avoided at all costs is the liberal position that,

> there was no certain knowledge of the temporal sequence, or that quite contradictory accounts existed, or that some source represented the events in a particular way, not because that was the way it happened, but because that was important for the theological message of that particular source.

For conservative Christians, including fundamentalists, it is important to sustain inerrancy by ironing out narrative inconsistencies, since the Gospels themselves are literary texts that aspire to narrative coherence. Herein lies an important difference between the Bible and the Koran. The holy text of Islam does not take the form of a narrative, nor is its structure chronological. The *suras* (chapters) are assembled approximately in order of length, with the shortest at the end and the longest (apart from the Opening) at the beginning. The sequence also corresponds, very roughly, to reverse chronological order: as you might find in a collection of letters or legal documents in a box-file, the oldest are at the bottom, the most recent near the top.

The Koran is presented by orthodox Islam as the very Words that God dictated to Muhammad from the beginning of his prophetic ministry (around 610) until his death in 632. Passages in the Koran that refer to historical events such as the Battle of Badr, Muhammad's first important victory against his pagan enemies in 634, are not self-explanatory. In order to understand the context of such passages and to make sense of many others, later generations of scholars had to refer to the secondary body of literature known as the Hadith, the originally oral reports of the Prophet's sayings and deeds as transmitted by his contemporaries. While the Koran is regarded by the vast majority of Muslims as the Word of God unmediated by human authorship, arguments about the authenticity of some individual Hadiths existed long before Western scholars trained in biblical studies began to cast their critical eyes upon the whole corpus.

Higher Critical scholarship of the Koran, using methodologies adapted from biblical criticism, is still largely confined to scholars working in Western universities. So sensitive is this area for Muslims that 'Ibn Warraq', a Muslim-born writer trained in Arabic who accepts the findings of radical Western scholarship, has felt it necessary to publish his work under a pseudonym. In the post-Rushdie atmosphere of cultural confrontation between Islamic and Western worlds, criticism of the Koran demands considerably more caution than criticism of the Bible. Even scholars working in Western universities have been denied tenure or promotion because of pressures from Muslim funders. Despite the pressures on critical scholarship, the challenge of subjecting the Koran to Higher Critical methods remains open. As with the Bible, the spotting of apparent anomalies or contradictions in the text can lead to the unravelling of the received understanding of the relationship between the text and the circumstances of its appearance.

At a rudimentary level the sceptical reader may ask how a text presumed to have been dictated by God or an angel acting for him contains passages (including the Opening, or *Fatiha*) which are clearly prayers or invocations addressed *to* the Almighty. Indeed, throughout the text there is uncertainty or ambiguity about who is addressing whom. As Richard Bell and Montgomery Watt argue in their scholarly *Introduction to the Quran*:

> The assumption that God is himself the speaker in every passage leads to difficulties. Frequently God is referred to in the third person. It is no doubt allowable for a speaker to refer to himself in the third person occasionally, but the extent to which we find the Prophet apparently being addressed and told about God as a third person is unusual. It has, in fact, been made a matter of ridicule that in the Quran God is made to swear by himself.

Aswith the Bible, there are issues about the integrity of the text of the Koran. The early Shia sectarians believed that passages favourable to Ali, whom they believed to have been passed over as Muhammad's rightful successor, were suppressed; whilst the puritanical Kharijis (seceders), who split from the mainstream body of Islam before even the Shia, could not believe that the Sura of Joseph, which other scholars have seen as a positive celebration of human sexuality, could rightfully belong in the holy book. Such views, of course, can be dismissed as reflecting the sectarian concerns of those holding them. More problematic are archaeological difficulties, including the orientation of the *qibla* (signalling the direction of prayer) in some of the earliest mosques, which point towards Jerusalem rather than Mecca.

On the basis of textual, archaeological, and non-Islamic sources such as the writings of Christian monks, a revisionist school of historiography based mainly in Britain and Germany has developed the bold hypothesis that rather than arising in Arabia (as the Koranic commentaries and biographies of Muhammad constructed

> [The revisionist scholars] regard the whole established version of Islamic history down at least to the time of Abd al-Malik (685–705) as a later fabrication, and reconstruct the Arab Conquests and the formation of the Caliphate as a movement of peninsular Arabs who had been inspired by Jewish messianism to try to reclaim the Promised Land. In this interpretation, Islam emerged as an autonomous religion and culture only within the process of a long struggle for identity among the disparate peoples yoked together by the Conquests: Jacobite Syrians, Nestorian Aramaeans in Iraq, Copts, Jews and (finally) Peninsular Arabs.
>
> (R. Stephen Humphreys, *Islamic History: A Framework for Inquiry*)

out of the Hadith literature relate), 'Islam' emerged as a new religious tradition out of polemics conducted between different factions of Semitic monotheists *after* the conquest of Palestine and the Fertile Crescent by Arabs from the peninsular.

The revisionists' historiography cannot be expected to leave the Koran untouched. John Wansbrough, architect of the revisionist school, argued that the Koran and the Hadith emerged out of sectarian controversies between Jewish and Christian monotheists over a long period, and were then 'projected back onto an Arabian point of origin'. A follower of this tendency, Gerald Hawting, draws on wide reading in the history of religions to suggest that Muhammad's attacks on polytheists, which are supposed to have occurred in Mecca, actually arose much later in the course of religious polemics between different groups of monotheists in the Levant. As a religious system, writes Hawting, 'Islam should be understood as the result of an intra-monotheist polemic, in a process similar to that of the emergence of the other main divisions of monotheism'.

Is a belief in the inerrancy of scripture a precondition of 'fundamentalism', a defining characteristic in all traditions? While it may be true that all Christian fundamentalists are inerrantists, the converse does not necessarily apply. Many Christian evangelicals who are not fundamentalists believe the Bible to be inerrant; while since the vast majority of believing Muslims are Koranic inerrantists, Islamic fundamentalism cannot really be defined in terms of Koranic inerrancy.

Since all fundamentalists in the Western monotheist traditions, Christianity, Islam, and (with some reservations) Judaism, may be considered textual inerrantists, a more limited or precise definition is needed if the Islamic radicals are to be included. The key family resemblance is to be found neither in literalism (which, as we have seen, is highly problematic) nor in inerrancy (much too broad) but in a common hermeneutic style. Christian and Muslim fundamentalists, and to a lesser degree their Jewish counterparts, share a religious outlook which, paradoxically, has many common features with the secularism or materialism they claim so adamantly to oppose. Rather than calling it 'literalist', I would prefer to describe this style as factualist or historicist.

In her discussion about fundamentalism in *The Battle for God*, Karen Armstrong explains the prevalence of fundamentalism in the three major Western religious traditions by suggesting that two sources of knowledge that were kept apart in pre-modern times, *mythos* and *logos*, the respective preserves of timelessness and constancy, have collapsed under the influence of modern religious ideologues, many of whom are trained in the 'hard' or applied sciences. They read religious texts as blueprints for practical action. In pre-modern times, according to Armstrong, people

> evolved two ways of thinking, speaking and acquiring knowledge, which scholars have called *mythos* and *logos*. Both were essential; they were regarded as complementary ways of arriving at truth, and each had its separate area of competence.

The old ideal had been to keep *mythos* and *logos* separate: political action was the preserve of reason.

The implication of Armstrong's analysis is that people in pre-modern societies were somehow less prone to take action on the basis of mythical ideas than in modern societies, while begging the question of what constitutes the modern. Her argument flies in the face of historical evidence that many pre-moderns (howsoever defined) enacted their myths in rational terms: the early conquests of Islam and the development of Islamic law, not to mention several eschatologically oriented movements throughout Islamic history, or similar movements in the history of Christianity and Judaism, furnish numerous examples.

A more fruitful approach to modern fundamentalisms would focus on the empowering dimensions of myths as self-validating expressions of the sacred in a pluralistic world in which real power and authority have become diffused and anonymous. As the sociologist Anthony Giddens reminds us, modernity is not so much characterized by faith in science (which, as the philosopher Karl Popper pointed out, always rests on shifting sands) but on trust in such anonymous abstract systems as the banking system or the depersonalized interactions between engineers, mechanics, pilots, and air traffic controllers that keep passenger jets flying. Trust in abstract systems provides for the reliability of day-to-day living, but by its very nature cannot supply either the mutuality or intimacy offered by relations of personal trust. The latter, as Giddens points out, can only be established through a process of self-enquiry since trust between individuals is based on mutual self-disclosure. The discovery of oneself becomes a project directly involved with the reflexivity of modernity. Hence in the United States, Buddhism, Sufism, and other religious traditions centred on 'discovery of the inner self' have become popular religious options.

Although on the face of it fundamentalist movements, with their highly authoritarian character, seem to run counter to this trend, closer inspection suggests there may be more similarity between modern 'fundamentalisms' and New Age cults or new religious movements than many observers suppose. Both provide sources of authority in a global environment where actual power is diffused and impersonal. Both can provide psychological reassurance in a world in which areas of relative security interlace with radical doubt and with disquieting scenarios of risk. Not all fundamentalist movements are political. Fundamentalist engagement in politics usually has local causes, not the least of which is the pursuit of power or influence by groups which consider themselves to have been disenfranchised politically or culturally.

While I would question Armstrong's assumption that pre-moderns always kept *mythos* and *logos* in balance, her point about the literalism, or rather the factualism, with which modern religious ideologues treat scripture, as manuals for practical action, as distinct from sources of personal inspiration or moral guidance, is well made. Research reveals that the majority of Islamist activists, including the civil engineer Osama bin Laden and the architect Mohamed Atta, are drawn not from people trained in theology or religious studies, but from the ranks of graduates in modern faculties such as medicine or engineering who combine a sophisticated knowledge of the technical products of modernity with two-dimensional understandings of their inherited faith tradition.

In the widest sense, all thought tends towards the mythical because of the way in which the human mind works. The mind is not a computer that dishes up individual words or factoids from a vast electronic memory, performing in seconds calculations that would have taken Einstein a lifetime or more. The mind works by drawing inferences from the data presented to it by jumping, as it were, to conclusions on the basis of very limited information. 'A description of our minds as a bundle of inference systems, differently activated by different objects, is better than that of a mental encyclopedia because it is much closer to the way a brain is actually organised', writes Pascal Boyer in *Religion Explained*, a book which brilliantly combines an anthropological approach to religion with recent discoveries in cognitive science and evolutionary biology.

Myths, like poetry, exploit our inference systems. They encapsulate thought rather than teasing or spelling it out logically. The philosopher Karl Jaspers saw myth as the 'first order of knowing'. Contrary to Auguste Comte, the philosopher of positivism, and Rudolf Bultmann, the theologian who believed that Christianity must be demythologized, Jaspers argued the case for myth as a source of creative power, a 'seedbed of metaphor, symbolism and ideas out of which later reflection and analysis have developed'. The great exemplars for using myth as a 'seedbed of symbolism' were Sigmund Freud and C. G. Jung. Freud found in the myth of Oedipus a way of encapsulating the paradoxes and complexities of human sexuality; Jung deployed myth as a means of exploring the archaeology of consciousness through the surfacing of religious symbols and archetypes in dreams.

Formally speaking, fundamentalists utterly reject the subjectivization of religion or its internalization into the private recesses of the self. A century before Jung, William Blake anticipated the Swiss psychoanalyst by insisting that 'all deities reside in the human breast'. 'Jesus was the Son of God', proclaimed Blake, 'but so am I, and so are you'. Yet Blake's mystical religiosity was not far removed from that of those born-again Christians who follow the moderate Southern Baptist theologian E. Y. Mullins in describing the conversion experience as 'falling in love with Jesus'. American fundamentalists do not reject the subjective, mythical 'Jesus of the heart' in their rebellion against modernism. Indeed, those millions of born-again Christians who claim to have taken Jesus as their personal saviour may come closer to Blake's heretical Gnosticism than most of them would care to admit. But they also demand the restoration of the historical Jesus along with an inerrant Bible that is true 'in all realms of reality' and 'all fields of knowledge', as the Statement on Scripture passed by the Southern

Baptist Convention following the fundamentalist victory in 1987 has it. The imagination, which Blake described as the 'Divine Body in Every Man', is fed and fructified by myth. But for fundamentalists, who take myth in its popular sense of 'lie', as distinct from an archetypical or elemental truth, myth must be collapsed into history – the record of things as they actually happened in the world of verifiable, external reality. And since the Bible contains a number of prophetic books, a literal or factualistic reading of it describes events that will occur in the foreseeable historical future.

The collapsing of myth into history is one of the clearest of the family resemblances by which different members of the fundamentalist tribe may be identified. Though prominent among premillennial Protestants, it is far from being confined to them. Sayyid Qutb, the Islamist ideologue who shaped the thinking of Osama bin Laden and most of today's Islamist groups, though a man of great literary sensitivity, urged his followers to approach the Koran as a manual for action, as distinct from a source of moral or spiritual guidance. He should approach it in order to act upon it immediately, 'as a soldier on the battlefield reads his daily bulletin so that he knows what is to be done'.

A similar collapsing of foundational myth into contemporary action informs Jewish extremism. In the Bible, the Children of Israel are commanded by God to massacre the Amalekites, an indigenous Caananite tribe, along with their women, children, and flocks. For fundamentalist militants such as Rabbi Yisrael Hess, formerly the campus rabbi of Tel Aviv's Bar-Ilan University, the Amalekites of scripture are assimilated to contemporary Palestinian Arabs. An article by the rabbi entitled 'The Commandment of Genocide in the Torah' ends with the chilling words: 'The day will yet come when we will all be called to fulfil the commandment of the divinely ordained war to destroy Amalek.' Biblical eschatology collapses past and future, putting history into reverse. For many American fundamentalists, the return of Christ will be preceded by the war against the Antichrist and the Days of Tribulation, when those who have not been saved will perish miserably in a series of catastrophic disasters. A popular version of the apocalyptic events predicted in the Book of Revelation, Hal Lindsay's *Late Great Planet Earth*, first published in 1970, has sold more than 30 million copies to date.

A small, but critical, step separates such predictions from their concretization or enactment. Most fundamentalists are content to let the divine will take its course, unaided by human intervention. But when the divine is actualized and brought onto the plane of history, humans become its self-appointed instruments. In Israel there have been several attempts by Jewish fundamentalists to destroy the Dome of the Rock and al-Aqsa Mosque, which were built on the site of the Second Temple destroyed by the Romans in 66 CE. At his trial on terrorist charges one of the plotters, Yehuda Etzion, challenged the competence of the Israeli court to sit in judgement over him: God had given him personal responsibility to advance the process of redemption through radical action. There is a registered association, the Faithful of Temple Mount, which demands that the Dome be levelled and the site purified by the slaughter of a flawless red heifer, as prescribed in the Bible, before the new temple is built. As pure red heifers are extremely rare, the association is funding a breeding programme in the United States with the aim of producing such an animal.

Messianic movements built around eschatological expectations are a constant of human history and potent engines of change. The future goal of a classless society to which the founders of modern communism aspired was rooted in a secularized version of Judaeo-Christian eschatology. There are close parallels in the Nazi idea of a Thousand Year Reich in which racially pure Aryans will rule most of the world. That history progresses teleologically towards a final eschatological denouement is fundamental to the Judaeo-Christian outlook. As several historians, including Christopher Hill and Norman Cohn, have shown, revolutionary movements in pre-modern times, such as the Fifth Monarchy Men of the English Revolution or the Anabaptists of Münster, were fuelled by chiliastic expectations and end-of-the-world scenarios. The communist and Nazi utopias drew deeply on these age-old eschatological ideas.

The difference between an eschatology predicated on supernatural intervention and one founded on human action may be slighter than one might think, for fundamentalist action involves, almost by definition, the appropriation of the divine will. As a Defender of God, the fundamentalist militant claims the right to act on his behalf. By collapsing myth into history, by taking action on God's behalf, the fundamentalist paradoxically affirms the supremacy of the human will. In Nietzsche's famous parable, a madman runs into the marketplace crying 'I seek God! I seek God!' – when the bystanders ask him where he imagines God has gone, the madman glares at them furiously: 'Where has God gone? . . . I mean to tell you. We have killed him, you and I! We are all his murderers!' In confusing God with their own will-to-power the fundamentalists may indeed be killing Him.

Chapter 4
Controlling women

On 4 October 1987 in the village of Deorala near Jaipur in Rajasthan, Roop Kanwar, a beautiful 18-year-old bride of less than eight months mounted the funeral pyre of Maal Singh, her 24-year-old husband who had died of gastroenteritis (or possibly committed suicide, after repeatedly failing his medical school entrance exams). Taking her dead husband's head in her lap, in the prescribed manner, Roop was burned alive. In her final moments one arm was seen to stretch out from the flames. Opponents of *sati* (who included the state authorities and some religious leaders) saw this as a gesture of defiance, or perhaps a desperate effort in her final seconds to escape. The crowd saw it as a benediction. There were hundreds of witnesses to this particular act of *sati*, which, unlike several previous episodes, attracted nationwide attention, partly because of the publicity given it by feminist protestors and other anti-*sati* groups.

Although the ritual burning of widows became illegal throughout India after the British governor of Bengal, Lord Bentinck, banned it in 1829, the practice has acquired iconic status as an act of spiritual sacrifice and like similar practices, such as dowry murders, female infanticide, and, latterly, the abortion of females when the sex of a foetus has been determined by amniocentesis, has proved difficult to eradicate. Thirty-seven people, three of them minors, were accused of abetting Roop Kanwar's illegal

4. *Sati* stone showing the hands of women who sacrifice themselves

immolation, including the bride's father-in-law and her brother, who lit the pyre. None of the indictments was successful because no one who attended the ceremony was prepared to risk prosecution under the Sati (Prevention of Glorification) Act by giving evidence in court. Within a year Roop Kanwar's shrine was attracting thousands of visitors. The money collected from voluntary donations amounted to more than 70 lakh rupees (more than $250 thousand), an immense sum in one of India's poorest districts. Despite laws enacted with the specific purpose of banning pro-*sati* propaganda in local and national elections, 4,000 visitors attended the anniversary of Roop Kanwar's *sati* in 1988. When the authorities stopped public transport from Deorala, the pilgrims arrived on foot, by camel cart or private buses crowded with people clinging to the roofs or hanging from the windows. More than 800 wayside booths appeared, selling souvenirs, snacks, toys, coconuts, and incense – along with the inevitable photo collages of the smiling Roop and her husband enveloped by flames.

Fundamentalism or tradition? Murder or suicide? The ultimate symbol of female oppression or an ironic, if extreme, demonstration of 'a woman's right to choose'? The questions raised by the *sati* of Roop Kanwar are not just significant in themselves: they concern our discussion of the F-word – its semantic biography. The Deorala bride's immolation seems to have been the occasion for its use in the context of Hinduism and its introduction into the lexicon of Indian English.

For its supporters, who included the weighty figure of Shankayracharya of Puri, one of the four pontiffs or heads of the Advaita religious tradition, *sati* is a profoundly spiritual act by which a woman achieves immortality for herself and her husband. By remaining at his side during the cremation, she shelters him from the spiritual dangers of death, cancelling any karmic shortcomings accrued during his lifetime, as well as offering benefits to those who witness her act. Like the Muslim suicide martyrs, the *sati's* family derives spiritual benefit from her act of sacrifice: the blessings she accrues are enjoyed by seven generations before and after her.

For its detractors, who include the Shankayracharya of Kanchipuram, *sati* is far from being a necessary part of Hindu tradition. According to this authority the philosopher, seer, and teacher Adi Shankara, from whom all the Shankayracharyas derive their spiritual authority, condemned the practice more than a thousand years before the British intervention. Feminist activists and writers see the practice as a ritualized instance of violence against women, as part of the spiritual nexus which enslaves Hindu women psychologically, encouraging abuse by denying their individuality and confining them to the household. For Sakuntala Narasimhan, a journalist and musician, *sati* is merely the most egregious in a raft of degrading practices to which Indian women are constantly subjected.

> Smothered or poisoned at birth, given away in marriage at a tender age, bargained over like some commodity by dowry-hungry in-laws, secluded in the name of chastity and religion, and finally burned for the exaltation of the family's honour, or shunned as inauspicious widows, the burden of oppression took different forms at different stages of a woman's life, from birth to death, in a chain of attitudes linked by contempt for the female.

Unlike the Abrahamic traditions of Judaism, Christianity, and Islam, there is no single text, such as the Bible or the Koran, identified with the Word of God or supreme religious authority in Hinduism. The Hindu scriptures consist of a massive body of texts dating back more than 4,000 years and added to over the centuries: the example, *par excellence*, of what scholars call 'cumulative tradition'. Claims that there are references to *sati* in the Rig Veda, one of the oldest of the Vedic texts, and the Mahabharata, the most famous of the Hindu epics, have been challenged by scholars who argue that the custom is of much more recent origin. *Sati* may be an invented patriarchal tradition that originated among the nobility (the Kshatriya class) rather than the priestly class of Brahmins, as a means of ensuring that their women were not violated by invading armies.

The Rajputs of Rajasthan, who take pride in their warrior traditions, encouraged their women to immolate themselves in a rite known as *jauhar* rather than submit to being raped by invaders. As John Stratton Hawley suggests, there is a close connection between *sati* and the memory of *jauhar* in Rajasthan. Sociologically, the defence of *sati* appears to be related to the rise of the Marwawi community, an important group of North Indian merchants whose homeland lies in the area around the town of Jhunjhunu in Rajasthan. The Great Queen Sati temple at Jhunjhunu, not far from Deorala, is the nation's largest and wealthiest *sati* temple, drawing tens of thousands of visitors each year. It commemorates the Rani Sati, a maternal manifestation of the divinity. As the 15-year-old bride of an unconsummated marriage, she was so dedicated to her husband that she chose *sati* rather than life as a widow. The cult of the Rani Sati reinforces the Marwawi clan's group identity, acting as the primary focus of their communal bond. The Jhunjhunu temple has inspired the construction of several *sati* temples in Delhi.

Despite the problematic use of the F-word outside the textually based Abrahamic religious tradition, at least two family resemblances suggest a relationship between the pro-*sati* movement in India and fundamentalisms in other religious traditions. The first, to be looked at more closely in the next chapter, is the politicization of religion and its relationship with nationalism, both cultural and political. The second is the closely related issue of gender. Politically, the Bharatiya Janata Party, which led India's governing coalition until 2004, was intimately involved in the pro-*sati* cause in Rajasthan, with one of its leaders, Vijayaraje Scindia, insisting that a voluntary act of self-immolation by a widow in dedication to her husband should not be allowed to constitute an offence in law. The head of the Janata Party in Rajasthan, Kalyan Singh Kalvi, responded to the criticism that *sati* demeans women by stating: 'In our culture, we worship the motherland, *dharma*, and *nari*, thereby making a direct connection between motherland, religion, and woman.'

Rather than being the defence of an exotic item of religious heritage threatened with extinction, the pro-*sati* agitation can be seen as part of a counter-feminist or 'patriarchal protest movement' that is common ground among fundamentalists in all traditions. In a pioneering study that looked in detail at two versions of religious fundamentalism – the original fundamentalism of early 20th-century America and the Shii Islamic version which came to power in Iran in 1979 – the sociologist Martin Riesebrodt saw both as aspects of a common patriarchal protest movement. Though he refrained from drawing wider conclusions, there is plenty of evidence to suggest that his approach can be applied to fundamentalisms not just in Iran and America, but in many other places currently being affected by politicized, public religiosity.

Several recent studies suggest that sex or, more specifically, the control of female sexuality looms large in the language employed by fundamentalists.

> The wave of animalism which is sweeping over the world today, and the degradation of the modern dance, the sensualism of the modern theatre, the glorification of the flesh in modern styles, and the sex suggestion of modern literature, the substitution of dogs for babies, the appalling divorce evil, have all come about because of this degrading philosophy of animalism which evolution is spreading over the earth.
>
> (J. R. Straton, *Searchlight*, 7/12, February 1924)

In the 1920s, American fundamentalists like John R. Straton explicitly linked the public expression of female sexuality to the corrosive effects of Darwinism, or what he preferred to call, polemically, 'animalism'.

Revolutionary Islamist groups like the Fedayan-i Islam denounce unveiled women in similar, if more dramatic, language: 'Flames of passion rise from the naked bodies of immoral women and burn humanity to ashes', causing young men to neglect their work. More than half the provisions of a 1981 law introduced in the Islamic Republic to codify Koranic prescriptions – 107 out of 195 articles – were concerned with sexual activities, ranging from the prosecution of adultery and homosexuality to preventing unrelated persons of the same sex lying naked under a blanket.

Reisebrodt sees the obsessive concern with sexuality common to American and Iranian fundamentalisms as a reaction to broader anxieties resulting from rural displacement and economic change. Fundamentalism, in his view, is a protest against the assault on patriarchal principles in the family, economy, and politics. The symptoms of patriarchal decline, he argues, manifest themselves primarily in the spheres of the family and sexual morality; but the underlying causes may lie in those very processes the sociologist Max Weber regarded as integral to modernity: the expansion of large-scale 'rationalized' operations, entailing formalized and codified relationships, at the expense of small businesses based on intimate paternalistic relations between employers and employees. In resisting such aspects of what Weber famously called 'the disenchantment of the world', fundamentalisms may appear to be anti-modern. But reality forces them to absorb many of modernity's salient features.

According to Riesebrodt, what fundamentalists cannot prevent in the way of structural transformation they attempt to impose symbolically. A gender-based division of labour is found in nearly all pre-modern societies. Under today's conditions it can no longer be sustained by traditional domestic arrangements, since in most modern societies women are required in the workforce. Instead, segregation is achieved by symbolic means such as sartorial coding – long hair and skirts for American women, with 'Christian' haircuts (short back and sides) for their menfolk; the veil in its various forms for Muslim women and the beard, a mark of sex and piety, for Muslim men. These forms of public religiosity may mask, but do not necessarily reverse or even delay, the processes of secularization.

Family values are fundamental to religious thought and behaviour in nearly all traditions. At times when social or political changes affect the family, religions are liable to react as though they are being undermined at their very foundations. However, given the varied social worlds in which fundamentalists actually operate, the results are far from being uniform. Nor are they necessarily reactionary or conservative.

In Latin America, where men often abandon their children, the patriarchal ideology promoted by evangelical churches encourages them to be more responsible fathers. Women, the voiceless group in the region, find in evangelical and Pentecostal communities the space and opportunity to exercise their gifts, while their husbands are encouraged to encounter a relational and affective part of themselves denied by the traditional 'macho' culture. Similarly, Japanese New Religions, some of which were founded by female prophets, theoretically reinforce ideals of male dominance while actually allowing women more active and participatory roles than traditional Buddhism and Shinto. In Sri Lanka, a women's Buddhist movement, the *dasa-sil-mata*, has campaigned to restore a long-defunct order of Buddhist nuns, against resistance from several male-dominated Buddhist organizations. Even in Iran, where many female workers were purged after the 1979 revolution, the situation is not unambiguous, as the revolution has encouraged the emergence of middle-class feminists determined to reinterpret Islam as empowering them rather than restricting their activities.

In the Islamic world particularly, the issue has been confused by the symbolism of the veil and its ambiguities. In the 20th century, women's emancipation in Egypt, Iran, and other Muslim countries was symbolized by the abandoning of the veil by upper-class women under the influence of Western culture, or in some cases its abolition by reforming autocrats. Abolished by decree by unpopular governments, the veil could easily be transformed into an emblem of cultural or political resistance. In Algeria, veiled Muslim women played an active part in the struggle for independence against France. In Egypt, observers have noted that the fundamentalist ideology which insists on veiling for women may actually reflect an emancipation from family bonds, rather than an endorsement of them. Young women who wear the *hijab* (veil or religious dress) no longer seek their parents' permission to visit mosques or attend religious meetings. Allah replaces the father as the ultimate authority for individuals, while stressing their obligations to the wider community.

At the same time, real horror stories abound. A recent example has been the fate of women in Afghanistan, a landlocked, mountainous country where patriarchal tribal customs have retained their hold for much longer than elsewhere. Among the Ghizlai, the women are secluded from non-*mahrams* —men other than fathers or brothers to whom they could be married. Among the Pushtuns, a bride who does not bleed on her wedding night may be killed by her father or brothers. 'Honour killings' for alleged sexual misconduct by women are far from being limited to mountainous, tribal regions: they occur in many other parts of the world, and though Jordan, Egypt, Syria, and Iraq furnish numerous examples, honour killings are far from being confined to Muslim societies. The culture of 'honour and shame', in which masculine honour and identity are predicated on female virtue, was until recently just as prevalent in Catholic Spain and Sicily, and the Orthodox Balkans, as it in Muslim lands.

Among the Afghani Pushtuns, however, the patriarchal structures are as rigid and confining to women as any on the planet. The

Pushtunwali – the Pushtun customary law – differs in signal respects from Islamic legal practice elsewhere. Divorce (a possibility in mainstream Islam, though easier for men than women) is prohibited and women are prevented from owning land (contrary to the provisions of normative Islamic law). Women are wholly regarded as the property of men and as pawns in economic and political exchanges, with marriages, enforced or otherwise, used as a way to end tribal feuds, to cement alliances between clans, or to increase a family's prestige. According to a well-known Pushtun saying, 'a woman is best either in the household or in the grave', with *purdah* (seclusion and veiling outside the household) regarded as a key element in protecting the family's pride and honour. Because of male resistance, over 90% of Afghan women remained illiterate until recently. (The current rate is still about 80% for women, compared with about 50% for men.)

The political oscillations afflicting Afghanistan since the turn of the 20th century have revolved very largely around the 'woman question' and the issue of female segregation. From the 1920s, governments in Kabul had strongly supported women's education. King Amanullah (reigned 1919–29), like his contemporary Reza Shah Pahlevi in Iran, urged women to come out of *purdah*. Heeding his advice, members of the Westernized elite took to wearing European clothes, with skirts to the knee and heads uncovered. When Amanullah was overthrown by conservative tribesmen in 1929, women were put back in *purdah* and forced to wear the *chadari* or *burqa*, the tent-like garment that covers the whole body, leaving only a small grille for the eyes. *Purdah* remained in force until 1959, when Prime Minister Daoud Khan announced the voluntary end of seclusion and removal of the veil. In the 1960s, mini-skirts began to appear in the capital and unveiled female television announcers became stars for the minority of (mainly urban) people with television sets. Nevertheless, unveiled, educated women encountered brutal opposition, with women wearing Western dress, including teachers and schoolgirls, having their exposed legs shot at or splashed with acid. Generally, the pattern was far from uniform, with considerable variation between cities, such as ultra-conservative Kandahar and more liberal Herat and Kabul.

In April 1978, the People's Democratic Party of Afghanistan (PDPA) seized power in a *coup d état*. The new socialist government, which included a number of women at senior level, immediately enacted changes in family law to improve the status of women while encouraging female education and employment. Massive spending on weddings, a major cause of poverty, was discouraged. A decree on marriage limited the size of dowries and forbade the exchange of women for cash or kind. Literacy classes, including compulsory classes for women, were established in rural areas. Inspired by socialist ideals and the considerable advances in education and women's emancipation that had taken place in the neighbouring Soviet republics of Central Asia, the new rulers of Afghanistan adopted a radical modernist outlook, one that linked Afghan backwardness to feudalism, widespread female illiteracy, and the exchange of girls.

All these measures encountered massive resistance from conservative tribal leaders. In Kandahar, female literacy workers were murdered. On at least two occasions, the men killed all the women in their families to prevent them from 'dishonouring' them. The new marriage rules enraged rural landowners, who regarded women as a form of currency in property exchanges. Compulsory education for girls raised the prospect that they might stop submitting to family (that is, male) authority. The Soviet invasion in 1979, intended to prop up the faction-ridden socialist government, sparked a vigorous and ultimately successful national resistance movement, backed by Saudi Arabia, Pakistan, and (clandestinely) by the United States. In what would become a global *jihad* (struggle or holy war) against the Soviet occupation, women were notably absent. Unlike most anti-colonial movements (including the Algerian struggle against France), Afghan women played virtually no part in the *jihad*. They were, however, conspicuous on the pro-Soviet side, with four out of seven militia commanders appointed to the communist Revolutionary Council being women.

> **Let us state what sort of education the UN wants. This is a big infidel policy which gives such obscene freedom to women, which would lead to adultery and herald the destruction of Islam. In any Islamic country where adultery becomes common, that country is destroyed and enters the domination of the infidels because their men become like women and women cannot defend themselves. Anybody who talks to us should do so within Islam's framework. The Holy Koran cannot adjust itself to other people's requirements. People should adjust themselves to the requirements of the Holy Koran.**
>
> (Maulvi Jalilullah Maulvizada, interviewed by Ahmed Rashid, June 1997)

When the ultra-conservative Taliban took over in 1996, after several years of civil strife and tribal conflict that followed the Soviet withdrawal in 1989, Afghanistan's gender war reached its nadir. Within three months of the capture of Kabul, the Taliban closed 63 schools in the Afghan capital, depriving more than 100,000 girls of education, along with 150,000 boys. They shut down Kabul University, sending home 10,000 students, of whom 4,000 were women. Female employees were stripped of their jobs, creating chaos in public health and social services. As many as 150,000 women may have been affected by the prohibitions on women's employment, including teachers, doctors, nurses, and civil servants. Sophisticated, educated urban women were forced to wear the *burqa*: decrees passed by the Taliban even banned the Iranian-style headscarf, or *chador*, as an unacceptable foreign fashion import.

The Taliban regime, which ended in October 2001, following America's aerial bombardment, is the most extreme example of a misogynistic, reactionary trend that is to be found throughout the developing world, especially in South Asia and the Middle East. But the trend is also strong in other countries where conservative versions of Islam hold sway. Although female education is encouraged by the state, Saudi women are still forbidden to drive motor vehicles (obliging them, ironically, to rely on the services of chauffeurs or taxi drivers to whom they are not related by blood or marriage, contrary to traditional norms). In a notorious episode that made international headlines in 2001, 15 girls at a boarding school in Jedda were burned to death when their dormitory caught fire. The religious police closed the gates on them because they had not covered themselves in accordance with the requirements of strict female modesty prevailing in the desert kingdom. As in some other Gulf states, Saudi women are not allowed to travel abroad unless accompanied by male relatives. Even in Sudan, where the National Islamic Front prides itself on its activist female cadres, a woman must have her brother or husband's permission when applying for a passport. In Pakistan, the Hudood ordinances passed by the military ruler General Zia al-Haqq, under fundamentalist pressure, effectively equated rape with adultery (*zina*), a crime which, though punishable by death in Islamic law, requires four independent adult male witnesses for its prosecution. The effect of this law has been to make it virtually impossible for a woman to press charges against a rapist without herself risking indictment for adultery.

What prompts women to sign up to religious movements that many would see as inimical to their interests? While generalizations are problematic, it appears that nearly all fundamentalist groups or churches studied by scholars reject legal steps to ensure equality between the sexes and typically exclude women from the senior ranks of religious leadership. All or almost all express concern about control of female sexuality. All draw strict boundaries between male and female realms. All are hostile to homosexuality, transvestism, and other behaviours that transgress these boundaries or blur the

'God-given' distinction between male and female. All profess to admire the chaste or virtuous woman while deriding the so-called 'free' or secular woman, whether the latter is seen as a manifestation of the godless hedonism of popular culture, or the product of alien Western lifestyles perceived as threatening to national identity.

It may be argued, of course, that all the major religions are fundamentally patriarchal, since they came into being at historical periods distant from our own when human survival was predicated on a strict division of male and female realms. As the hero Arjuna tells the God Krishna in the *Baghavad Gita*:

> In overwhelming chaos, Krishna,
> Women of the family are corrupted,
> And when women are corrupted,
> Disorder is born in society.

In the languages of Islam, the word *fitna*, 'strife', is applied both to the early dissentions and civil wars that afflicted the primitive Islamic community after the death of the Prophet Muhammad, and the social strife that is seen to be the inevitable consequence of female unchastity. Orthodox Judaism, like Islam, preserves ancient taboos on menstruation, while women are seen as inferior to the extent that they are exempted from the primary religious duty of studying the Torah and Halakha. In the Genesis story, common to Judaism and Christianity, it is Eve, the weaker moral vessel, who is created from Adam's rib and who, beguiled by the serpent, tempts Adam to sin. St Augustine, the most influential of the early church fathers, irons out the contradictions in Genesis and Paul to make the case for female inferiority. Feminist theologians in all the Abrahamic traditions have found ways of re-reading the scriptures in order to demonstrate that the original texts are less misogynistic than they appear, that androcentric readings are false or narrowly partisan, and that alternative feminist readings have equal validity. Such efforts, however, while enabling women believers to participate more fully in religious activities previously reserved for men, are not in themselves sufficient to explain the appeal that fundamentalist versions of religion have for women.

In the first place, one should not underestimate the attraction that charismatic male preachers have for female followers. In the Pentecostal tradition, preachers such as Jimmy Swaggart (before his fall from grace after a much-publicized encounter with a prostitute) project a powerful image of masculinity that is consistent with the 'macho', militant style of Christianity proclaimed by preachers such as Billy Sunday.

> Jesus Christ intended his church to be militant as well as persuasive. It must fight as well as pray . . . The prophets all carried the Big Stick . . . Strong men resist, weaklings compromise . . . Lord save us from off-handed, flabby-cheeked, brittle-boned, weak-kneed, thin-skinned, pliable, plastic, spineless, effeminate, sissified, three-caret Christianity.
>
> (Billy Sunday, *Evening Times* (Trenton, NJ), 6 January 1916)

A more measured and sober figure like Jerry Falwell may appeal to female followers for his fatherly appearance. Television encourages this, for while God the Father cannot be seen on camera, mature and pleasant-looking men who speak on his behalf, such as Falwell and Pat Robertson, may provide iconically satisfying substitutes. Authoritative Muslim divines, such as Sheikh Yusuf al-Qaradawi, who has a regular slot on the al-Jazeera TV channel based in Qatar, are immensely popular with female viewers; while Osama bin Laden, vilified by the West as the leader of the al-Qaeda terrorist organization, has carefully made himself into an icon, modelled on the Prophet Muhammad – an image that may exercise a powerful appeal to Muslim women.

5. Militants displaying a poster of Osama bin Laden

But there are also more practical, down-to-earth reasons why women may be drawn to fundamentalist movements. Part of the appeal may be economic: in America, for example, although most women can support themselves by their own labour, most of the jobs available to women are less well paid than men's, suggesting that even in an advanced industrial society, women may live at a higher level when solely supported by a male.

Fundamentalist emphasis on family values, with women seen primarily in their capacity as mothers, wives, and homemakers, is perceived as having an element of economic realism – that is, legitimating and sanctifying an economic inevitability. In the developing world economic realism may be reinforced by cultural nationalism and anti-colonial sentiment. In Islamic countries, the *hijab* in its various guises proclaims a symbolic rejection of Western cultural and economic power (while affording a tacit acceptance of its benefits). Here the dislocating effects of industrialization and rapid urbanization affect men and women equally. While the general message of a return to 'tradition' as the key to the ills of dislocation and disempowerment is as readily accepted by women as by men in Islamic countries, the veil, as an invented or reinvented tradition, accommodates changing economic realities by enabling women to work without inviting the unwelcome attentions of men. Where veiling is compulsory, as in post-revolutionary Iran, fundamentalist readings of the legal texts may serve to commoditize and fetishize women by focusing obsessively on their sexuality and reproductive potential. Where it is espoused voluntarily, as among many young Muslims living in Western countries, the message it conveys may be the exact opposite. By concealing her body from the stranger's gaze, the wearer proclaims that she is not a sexual object to be judged by her physical appearance.

In a confused, and confusing, world in which gender roles are changing or under constant review, the sexual bipolarity encouraged by fundamentalists everywhere may be reassuring. Fundamentalism addresses the competing claims of children and career by seeming to authenticate motherhood, giving it priority over the feminist goal of human self-development. Its values may offer women a vision of financial and social security, provided they toe the line drawn by male religious leaders. The religious activities fostered by fundamentalism may facilitate female networking, providing fundamentalist women with the kind of gender solidarity or sisterly support to be found, for example, in feminist group activities. In Western countries, the encouragement by conservative politicians of 'family values', along with church-based charitable activities, lightens the burden of welfare carried by the taxpaying citizen, thereby restricting (in rhetoric, if not always in reality) the reach of the state over civil society. In the Americas especially, fundamentalism as well as some versions of non-fundamentalist evangelicalism, such as Robert Schuller's 'theology of self-esteem', acts as a liberation theology of the right, lending a sense of empowerment to people (particularly females) who had felt themselves threatened or marginalized in a culture addicted to hedonistic self-gratification and sexual profanity.

It would be wrong to underestimate the appeal of fundamentalism for women in societies where issues such as teenage pregnancy, AIDS, and drug abuse are matters of public concern. In old Europe such issues are primarily regarded as the concern of local or national government. In *laissez-faire* America, where the state is less committed to social spending and less inclined to intervene in the operation of market forces, old-fashioned Puritan virtue, rooted in America's founding mythology, retains a powerful appeal. Prosperity theology, implicit in the images of comfortable, middle-class Christians that appear on popular television shows such as Pat Robertson's *700 Club* or Robert Schuller's *Hour of Power* becomes explicit when television preachers finance their ministries by direct appeals for funds. The telethons to which viewers of Christian programming are regularly exposed show heart-warming stories of people who pledge their 15 dollars a month for Jesus, despite desperate financial circumstances. The promised rewards are not in heaven, but in earthly bank accounts: for those who make the pledge, previously sluggish investments suddenly yield handsome dividends, the unemployed partner in Christ suddenly lands a well-paid job. Reversing centuries of Christian teachings on poverty, prosperity theology reveals the secular, this-worldly heaven in store for born-again Christians. As the economically more vulnerable section of society, women may be especially susceptible to a message that promises tangible rewards for virtue and abstinence.

Similar considerations, modified to suit different cultural conditions, apply in the Islamic world, where the welfare organizations run by Islamist or fundamentalist movements, such as the Gamaat al-Islamiya in Egypt or Hamas in Palestine, are often better equipped to address the plight of desperately needy people than the corrupt bureaucrats of the government or regional authority. Women who sign up to the movement may be rewarded morally and materially: they receive the respect accorded to the 'mothers of the believers' while benefiting from the organization's welfare programmes. In Islam as in Protestantism and Judaism, God may be seen to reward those who abide by His rules.

There is, of course, a negative side to this picture. The benefits of sexual virtue are purchased at a formidable moral cost. In the polarized, Manichaean world of fundamentalist discourse, virtue is not enough. The enemies of God must be demonized. The 'loose' woman is an agent of Satan. In numerous fundamentalist tracts, 'family values' are a code-word for virulent homophobia. Fundamentalist fears of homosexuality have now crossed the Atlantic, infecting the Church of England, in which a significant proportion of clergy is gay. One diocesan bishop is even on record as claiming that homosexuality is caused by demons in the anus. In the summer of 2003 the appointment of Dr Jeffrey John, an openly gay clergyman, as Bishop of Reading, and his subsequent withdrawal under pressure from bishops in Africa and evangelicals within the Church, became a major source of controversy, threatening a permanent split in the Anglican Communion.

Similar trends are found in the world of Islam, where the traditional tolerance of homosexuality as being less threatening to family values than heterosexual (especially female) infidelity is now being replaced by active homophobia, with homosexuality wrongly stereotyped as an imported Western vice. Fresh from their all-male seminaries, the Taliban who ruled in Afghanistan executed homosexuals by lapidation, bulldozing walls to crush their bodies. In Iran, after the revolution, homosexuals were hanged; in Egypt,

6. A veiled Muslim woman casting her vote

under fundamentalist pressure, discos frequented by gays have been closed down and participants arrested.

In all such instances, fundamentalist concern to maintain the family as a social unit and transmitter of conservative values has been overtaken by a neurotic obsession with correct sexual behaviour. Space does not allow for a lengthy speculation into the causes of fundamentalist homophobia: but it seems obvious that self-repression and fear of one's own inner demons or sexual impulses may have much to do with it. When homoerotic feelings clash with the heterosexual values formally endorsed by religion, homophobia (directed against those who acknowledge and give expression to such forbidden sentiments) provides an all too obvious and easy way out.

While homophobia may be a largely male obsession, the mantra of 'family values' holds an obvious appeal for women, who find themselves competing on unequal terms in an increasingly competitive global environment. In the less privileged reaches of Western societies, the priority they give to their religious life enables such women to deal with the contradictions they experience in a world in which self-esteem is supposed to be achieved through work, but employers do not facilitate child-care or deal with the female body as normative. While public rhetoric may insist that family values are paramount, actual commitments to parenting are not always valued. Their overarching religious commitment and the female support fundamentalist women find in their churches make it easier for them to cope with lives that are full of tensions and difficulties. The very emphasis on male authority in congregational and domestic life has its advantages for such women. Marriage is valued, sexual fidelity demanded, drinking and carousing – traditional male pursuits – are discouraged. Fundamentalist men are expected to take an active part in bringing up their children. As Frances Fitzgerald observed: 'To tell Dad that he made all the decisions might be a small price to pay to get the father of your children to become a respectable middle-class citizen.'

Viewed from this perspective, female fundamentalism, which is found in all traditions, may be a transitional phase between the world in which women were largely confined to the home and one in which they fully participate in public and business life. Anita Weiss, who has worked with Muslim women in a traditionalist social milieu in Lahore, Pakistan, concludes that while the men view their womenfolk as being more capable than in the past, they also feel threatened by the potential of uncontrolled, educated, and economically independent women to compromise their honour and therefore their status among other men. Fundamentalisms are dynamic movements in the contemporary social landscape. Though conservative, they are far from being static. Nor are they invariably reactionary. By formally accepting male authority when moving into public arenas previously the preserve of males, fundamentalist women hope to soothe men's anxieties while quietly taking over their jobs.

Chapter 5
Fundamentalism and nationalism I

> The New Englanders are a People of God settled in those places
> which were once the Devil's territories ... a People here
> accomplishing the promise of old made unto our Blessed Jesus, that
> He would have the Utmost parts of the Earth for His possession.
>
> (Cotton Mather, New England Puritan)

The Puritan settlers in America would not have seen themselves as
'fundamentalists' since the term had not yet been invented.
Fundamentalism only comes into being when challenged by
modernist theologies, when post-Enlightenment scholarship is
perceived as threatening to the eternal verities enshrined in the
Word. But the American Puritans were fundamentalist in a broader
sense, in that they understood the portions of the Bible in a way that
differed significantly from most of their Old World counterparts.
Whereas Bunyan's *Pilgrim's Progress* would express the Puritan
spirit allegorically, his 'City of Destruction' and 'Slough of Despond'
being convincing depictions of psychological states in the
wilderness of this world, the American pilgrim experienced his
biblical narratives concretely, especially the Book of Exodus, which
charts the deliverance of the Children of Israel out of Egypt. There
is a one-to-one correspondence between miraculous crossing of the
Red Sea by the Israelites led by Moses, and the *Mayflower*'s perilous
journey across the Atlantic. The New Jerusalem promised in the
Book of Revelation – a spiritual aspiration for William Blake – was

for Joseph Smith, the Mormon Prophet, a Zion of bricks and mortar where the Kingdom of God acquired material form.

'The destiny of the American People is to subdue the continent, to unite the world in one social family', wrote William Gilpin, Governor of Colorado Territory, in 1846. 'Divine task! Immortal mission! America leads the host of nations as they ascend to this order of civilization . . . the industrial conquest of the world.' It is not customary to speak of 'American nationalism', but there can be little doubt that the fundamentals of Christianity, as they came to be understood by evangelical Protestants early in the 20th century, were closely bound up with the construction of a core WASP (White Anglo-Saxon Protestant) identity that sought to preserve itself from dissolution by external influences, ranging from imported German scholarship, Catholic immigration, and socialism, equated with communism – not to mention the profane cultural influences emanating from Hollywood, which was seen by conservatives as being dominated by emancipated, non-religious Jews. On the domestic front, moreover, most fundamentalists avoided having to engage in social interaction with the descendants of African slaves. The fundamentalist Southern Baptist Convention (comprising some 40,000 independent churches) is overwhelmingly white; while Bob Jones University, a fundamentalist educational bastion, still applies archaic rules against mixed racial dating. While some scholars see fundamentalism and nationalism as rival ideologies, in America, as in Israel, the movements are often barely distinguishable. Steve Brower comments:

> 'Faith in the Nation' though it still resonates through socially conservative, militarily-connected networks inside and outside the United States, has been appropriated in a symbolic sense by the fundamentalists. It justifies their role in realising global evangelization and revitalizing Americanism.

American fundamentalists perceive no conflict between religion and patriotism. Like their Puritan predecessors, they identify

America with Israel as a land covenanted to God's People on condition that they followed God's laws. The televangelist Pat Robertson (who unsuccessfully stood as a candidate for the Republican presidential nomination in 1987) is quite explicit about this identification. Since the Supreme Court 'insulted God' by banning prayer in school, he rants, America has been defeated in war, one president has been assassinated and another forced to resign, foreign powers have amassed huge surpluses in their trade with America, and the country is mired in debt. Since the Supreme Court 'legalized murder' by extending abortion rights, the country has been at the mercy of the OPEC oil cartel, American children have been 'victimized by marijuana, heroin, hallucinogens, crack cocaine, glue, PCP, alcohol, unbridled sex, a pop music culture that has destroyed their minds, the occult and Hindu holy men, and an epidemic of disease'. Only a return to God can save the nation.

Despite the very different social and political contexts of America and the Islamic worlds, the arguments are very similar to those deployed by Islamist writers and preachers. The Prophet Muhammad, according to the Islamists, triumphed over his enemies through battle as well as by preaching. Building on his victories as well as his obedience to God, his successors, the Rightly Guided Caliphs, conquered most of West Asia and North Africa as well as Spain. In this view, the truth of Islam was vindicated on the plane of real-time history, through its historical achievement in creating what would become a great world civilization. Islamists attribute the decline of Islam directly to loss of faith by Muslims, and especially to Muslim rulers who do not rule in accordance with Islamic law. If Muslims and leaders return to the straight path of righteousness ordained by God, the social and political decline that resulted in colonialism and the shabby, corrupt postcolonial order will be reversed. Far from being counternationalist, as argued by some scholars and ideologists, the fundamentalist argument that God rewards righteousness in terms of national success and this-worldly prosperity is one that chimes in perfectly with nationalist aims.

Theoretically, fundamentalism and nationalism are ideological opponents. In the formal discourses of writers such as Abul Ala Mawdudi, one the most influential Islamist writers, religion stands at the polar opposite of nationalism and all that nationalism stands for. Nationalism, for Mawdudi, promotes popular sovereignty or the will of the people expressed through secular institutions such as parliaments or national assemblies which legislate for the nation. 'The principle of the Unity of God', he wrote, 'altogether negates the concept of the legal and political sovereignty of human beings, individually or collectively God alone is sovereign and His commandments are the Law of Islam'. Mawdudi's opposition to nationalism was not just based on the fear that the Indian Muslim community from which he came would be discriminated against or suffer loss of identity in a Hindu-majority state. He was equally opposed to Muslim nationalisms, which he saw as being as reprehensible in the view of the Sharia law of God as Indian nationalism.

In Arab countries especially, the Islamist movements are ideological competitors of Arab nationalists. They aim to replace them in government, whether by winning elections (as in Algeria in 1991) or by armed rebellion, as happened in the Egyptian city of Assiut following the assassination of President Anwar Sadat in October 1981 and in the Syrian city of Hama, where at least 10,000 people were killed after a rebellion by the Muslim Brotherhood in 1982. Islamist ideologues routinely denounce their nationalist competitors or rulers as 'infidels' or 'man-worshippers', as usurpers who have substituted man-made laws instead of instituting the rule of God. The theocracies they advocate are supposed to be incompatible with human government.

In practice, the situation is rather more complicated. Historically, nationalisms in Europe emerged with the rise of urban autonomy and the 'emancipation of the bourgeoisie' from feudal bonds, sometimes in alliance with monarchs against landed aristocracies, sometimes against them. Both the French and American

7. The trial of the accused assassins of President Anwar Sadat of Egypt, 1981

revolutions generated nationalist forces by extending bourgeois freedoms, with all the rights of citizenship, to the whole of society (though not, in America's case, to slaves). In France, as in Russia after 1917, the revolution took a radically anti-clerical turn, because of the Church's strong identification with the discredited *ancien régime*. After 1792, the French Revolution, with its popular assemblies, processions, and fêtes, began exporting its patriotic ideals throughout Europe. Napoleon's conquests catalysed the forces of nationalism in Europe by provoking patriotic responses in Britain, Spain, Germany, Poland, and Russia, if not in Italy, where the anti-papal nationalism of the Risorgimento took much longer to emerge.

It would be wrong, however, to see nationalism as being uniformly anti-religious and secular. Everywhere nationalisms have been permeated by religious symbols, especially in places where the core identities that came to constitute nationhood had been buttressed by religious differences. The different identities that make up Britain were sustained by Presbyterianism in Scotland, non-conformity in Wales, and Catholicism in Ireland (excepting the North), just as Polish and Croatian identities were sustained by Catholicism; Greek and Serb identities by Eastern Orthodoxy; Malayan (or Malaysian) by Islam; Tibetan, Thai, and Sri Lankan identities by Buddhism. Yet for every case where national and religious allegiances seem to run in tandem, there are also contradictions. The Russian patriotism that gloried in the achievements of Peter the Great at a time of incipient industrialization and capitalism, also contained Slavophile elements which harked back to pre-Petrine Muscovy and its Orthodox monastic ways. The movement for Greek independence from the Ottomans, inspired by the French Revolution and Romantics such as Byron, combined two contradictory elements: a bourgeois constituency of merchants and intelligentsia who sought to revive the glories of ancient Athens; and a pious stratum among the Orthodox clergy and peasants who yearned for the recovery of Constantinople and the Byzantine Empire.

The ideal Islamic order aspired to by modern Islamist ideologues, including Abbassi Madani, the principal leader and founder of the Islamic Salvation Front (Front Islamique de Salut (FIS)) in Algeria, the Saudi dissident Osama bin Laden and the followers of the late Sheikh Taqi al-Din al-Nabahani, founder of the Islamic Liberation Party, Hizb al-Tahrir, corresponds to the classical concept of the Caliphate. In the Arab case, defeat at the hands of Israel in successive wars helped to popularize the quest for lost grandeur, a compensatory mechanism, perhaps, for failure on the battlefield. The revival of the Islamist movement in Egypt, quiescent during the heyday of Gamal Abdul Nasser, dates from Egypt's catastrophic defeat by Israel in 1967 – the moment when the modernist agenda behind his brand of secular Arab nationalism with its socialist orientation was discredited. But to state that the Arab nationalism articulated by Nasser and the Islamism or fundamentalism of bin Laden, Madani, and Nabahani are ideologically distinct does not mean that they are mutually exclusive or incompatible. In the Islamic world especially, nationalisms and fundamentalisms bleed into each other and overlap.

Islamic religious leaders were at the forefront of the nationalist or patriotic movements that resisted European colonialism in the 19th and 20th centuries, and in most cases threw it off after the Second World War. Such movements were not nationalist in the European sense, but they could be described as nationalistic, based as they were on the impulse to liberate their societies from foreign domination or governance.

Before European colonialism divided the whole world into discrete territorial units whose frontiers were often determined by arrangements among themselves, Islamic polities were organized communally rather than territorially. States were not bounded by lines drawn on maps. The power of a government did not operate uniformly within a fixed and generally recognized area, as happened in Europe, but rather radiated from a number of urban centres with a force which tended to grow weaker with distance and with the existence of natural or human obstacles. Patriotism was focused, not as in Renaissance Italy, England, or Holland, on the city, city-state, or nation in the modern territorial sense, but on the clan or tribe within the larger unit of the Umma, the worldwide Islamic community. Local solidarities were reinforced by practices such as marriage between cousins, a requirement in many communities. Clan loyalties were further buttressed by religion, with tribal leaders justifying their rebellions or wars of conquest by appealing to the defence of true Islam against its infidel enemies.

An example is that of the 'fundamentalist' Ibn Saud, a tribal leader who conquered, and united, most of the Arabian peninsular between 1904 and 1926 in alliance with a movement for religious reform founded by an 18th-century cleric, Muhammad ibn Abd al-Wahhab. The Wahhabi movement, which is still highly influential, thanks to the petro-dollars it receives from its Saudi patrons, is counternationalist in the sense that it sees its mission as universal and does not confine itself within the territorial boundaries of the Saudi state. Like other fundamentalist movements such as the Muslim Brotherhood (with whom it forged close ideological ties from the 1960s), it aims to revitalize the whole of the Umma along Wahhabi fundamentalist lines. But in a broader sense, it conforms to what Mark Juergensmeyer prefers to call 'religious nationalism' (rather than fundamentalism). Just as secular nationalism is far from being devoid of religious content, so religious nationalism is primarily political.

Juergensmeyer does not see nationalism as the ideological or polar opposite of fundamentalism, but rather as its complement or variant. He regards secular nationalism as itself having many of the characteristics of a religion, including doctrine, myth, ethics, ritual experience, and social organization. Both serve the ethical function of providing an overarching framework of moral order, a framework that commands ultimate loyalty from those who subscribe to it. The strongest parallel, he concludes, lies in the ability of nationalism and religion, alone among all forms of allegiance, to give moral sanction to martyrdom and violence.

The interconnected, overlapping relationship between secular and religious nationalisms is particularly evident where Islamist movements have taken power or come close to exercising it. In Algeria, the Islamic Salvation Front (FIS) was forced underground after the army intervened in December 1991 to prevent it from winning the second round of the national elections. Prior to its dismantling, the Front was a coalition of two main groupings: the *salafi* group, whose leaders were mostly educated through the medium of Arabic in Algeria or outside the country in the Arab East or English-speaking countries; and the Francophone al-Jazara group, or Algerianists, who were considered more open to modernist influences. Both factions were united in their desire to establish a state based on a restoration of the Islamic law, although al-Jazara offers a much less rigid reading of Islam than the *salafi* school, which is attached to the spirit and the letter of the Koran. Both groups rejected democracy as *kufr* (disbelief), and as a concept that is semantically alien to the spirit and texts, both sacred and secular, of Islam. (The objection is identical to that advanced by Jewish fundamentalists, who regard democracy as being Greek and hence alien.) The denunciations of democracy by FIS leaders was one of the pretexts the army was able to use for the overthrow of President Chadli Benjadid after the FIS victory at the polls in November 1991. One of the main beneficiaries of the army's action, which unleashed a cruel and bloody civil war that is said to have cost at least 100,000 lives, were Hamas (not to be confused with the Palestinian movement of the same name) and Nahda, two moderate Islamist parties that shared the cultural aims of FIS but were prepared to work within the system. The divisions among the Islamists enabled President Zeroual and his successor Abd al-Aziz Bouteflika to reintroduce limited democracy with a measure of Islamist support.

The merging of Islamist and 'Algerianist', or nationalist, currents in Algeria is consistent with patterns in many other Arab countries where the Islamist movements are challenging authoritarian or military-based regimes. Theoretically, in its 'pure' or ideal-typical forms, Islamism may present itself as an ideological alternative to nationalism, which it sometimes describes as a manifestation of *kufr*. But as in Ireland, where nationalists are almost invariably Catholic and loyalists invariably Protestant, the realities are much more complex. Opposition forces, whether nationalist or Islamist, feed on common discontents and manifest a common desire for a more authentic national culture. In their militant forms they exhibit the same intolerance for lifestyles deemed to be immoral or imported. Both attack the corruption of the military-backed regimes they seek to supplant. Both attack nationalisms they regard as discredited. But while challenging the old-style nationalism of the incumbent elites, Islamists adopt many of their assumptions.

Islamists all agree that Muslim societies should be governed in accordance with the divine (Sharia) law. However, they differ among themselves as to the forms that the Sharia should take under modern conditions. In striving to execute their agenda, they tend to rely on an undeclared modernist premiss: whereas in pre-modern or pre-colonial times the writ of government in Muslim countries was relatively weak, with the Islamic law administered by the class of religious scholars known as the *ulama* (the learned) under the authority of the ruler who was himself, in theory, subject to its provisions, the modern Islamists 'hold the state responsible for the deviation of the Muslim community when it is not Islamic, and consider it the instrument of its salvation when it is'. As Laura Guazzone points out, reference to the state as the central framework of Islamist political thinking and action constitutes a signal departure from theories of government developed during the classical age of Islam. It is clearly the result of dialectics with the cultural antagonists of Islamism, liberalism, nationalism, and socialism and of the engagement of the Islamist movements in *national* political processes.

The results are paradoxical. Where Islamists have actually held power – as (briefly, at municipal level) in Algeria, in Iran since the 1979 Islamic revolution, and in Sudan since 1989 – it is the postcolonial state and the interest groups controlling it that have benefited, rather than civil society. The rhetorical appeal of political Islam as representing 'freedom, under God, from the dominion of man over man' – the source of its capacity to mobilize people against tyrannical regimes – produces Machiavellian pragmatism that can prove to be no less corrupt or authoritarian than the system it replaces. The new regime's stated priorities may change from promising economic development and increasing prosperity to defending private virtue and public morality. The shift in emphasis from economics to morality may be to the advantage of free enterprise while appealing to the values of recently urbanized rural immigrants and the religiously observant middle class of small businessmen and shopkeepers, the two groups which constitute the backbone of Islamist support. In the case of Iran, and to a lesser extent the Sudan, the Islamist conquest of the state may have increased political participation, by enfranchising previously excluded or marginal groups. But far from diminishing the purchase of an oppressive authoritarian state over society, the Islamists have achieved the opposite, intentionally or otherwise. The shift from state control over the economy to state enforcement of social morality involves no diminution in the state's actual power, but rather the reverse.

The most explicit statement of this paradox appears in a letter the Ayatollah Khomeini wrote in January 1988, shortly before his death, to the man who succeeded him as the Supreme Guide of the Islamic Republic, the then President Ali Khamenei. Khomeini ruled that the power of the Islamic Republic was comparable to that enjoyed by the Prophet Muhammad himself. It was thereby permitted to take any measures in the interests of the Islamic state even where these might conflict with Islamic law as traditionally interpreted, including the religious obligations of prayer, fasting during the holy month of Ramadan, or Hajj (pilgrimage to Mecca). By giving the state priority over Islamic law, Khomeini revealed his true colours. Far from being a traditionalist, he established the theological ground for a radical break in the traditional relationship between Islam and the state, according to which the ruler was supposed to govern in accordance with what God sent down (that is, the Koran and the legal system derived from it) and to subject himself to these laws. In post-Khomeini Iran, state power is as formidable as it was before 1979 during the authoritarian regime of the Shah. Students, writers, and politicians who have dared to challenge the clerical rule have been harassed, tortured, imprisoned, and in some cases sentenced to death.

Far from being counternationalist in the sense of opposing the secular national states imposed on the Islamic world since decolonization, Islamism in practice mostly reveals itself as an alternative variety of nationalism whose political focus is cultural and religious rather than primarily economic (although Islamists do have some economic theories such as interest-free banking, which have been implemented in some Muslim countries, with varied degrees of success). In the Palestinian territories occupied by Israel since 1967, the Islamist groups Hamas and Islamic Jihad have shown more nationalist fervour than the more secular-oriented Palestinian Liberation Organization (PLO) by engaging in acts of terror, such as suicide bombings in metropolitan Israel, specifically aimed at sabotaging the peace process, in which the PLO has been engaged. In Pakistan, the Islamist Jamaat-i-Islami was fervently nationalistic in supporting the army's brutal campaign (which involved the systematic mass rape of Bengali women by soldiers mainly from the Punjab) against the secessionist movement in East Pakistan that resulted in the formation of Bangladesh.

There remains a contradiction between the utopian aim of a restored universal Islamic caliphate shared by supporters of Osama bin Laden and the reality of the national state. In practice, the logic of circumstances and the interplay of local ethnicities and regional rivalries ensure that the energies of Islamist movements are directed towards the attainment of power within existing Muslim states or communities.

Chapter 6
Fundamentalism and nationalism II

'The object of every national movement is only the seeking for its god, who must be its own god, and the faith in him as the only true one. God is the synthetic personality of the whole people taken from its beginning to its end', wrote Fyodor Dostoyevsky in *The Possessed*. The same insight informs the religious sociology of Émile Durkheim, who equated the sacred with the spirit of community, a projection of the communal spirit onto a supernatural, transcendental Being. Like religious communities, the nations are collectivities that transcend the sum of their individual parts; like religious communities, nations bear witness to the idea that human blood must be shed in their defence: the war memorials, cenotaphs, and tombs to the 'Unknown Warrior' that grace our cities attest to transcendental demands the nation makes of its citizens. Such demands, as Anthony Smith points out, are made on the basis of faith rather than empirical evidence.

> For nationalists, the nation, whatever the acts committed in its name, is essentially and ultimately good, as the future will reveal; the conviction of its virtue is not a matter of empirical evidence, but of faith.

Nationalist rhetoric everywhere is suffused with religious symbolism and purpose. The biblical story of Exodus exercised a powerful influence on the construction of American identities, from the Pilgrim Fathers to the New Zions (Nauvoo, Illinois, and Salt Lake City, Utah) founded by the Mormon Prophet Joseph Smith and his successor Brigham Young (the 'American Moses') in the American West during the 1840s. Taken to heart by Bible-loving Protestants, the Exodus myth has buttressed the group identities of Scottish-Irish Protestants in Ulster and Afrikaners in Southern Africa. In addition to the familiar enactment or exploitation of this myth by European Protestants, Anthony Smith has shown how the biblical idea of a 'chosen people' modelled on the Israelites was a vital component in the outlook of peoples as diverse as Ethiopians and Armenians.

For Jews, the Exodus narrative is not just treated historically but ritualized and given a spiritual meaning. According to Rabbi Sybil Sheridan, all Jews at the Seder table at Passover 'are to think of the Exodus as if they too were in Egypt at that time, and all are understood to have stood at the foot of Mount Sinai and been witness to the theophany that there took place'. It is not so much the event in itself that is central to the belief, but its meaning and the reinforcement of meaning through symbols and celebrations, especially in orthodox Judaism, which tends to approach history (or, to be more accurate, historical mythology) thematically rather than 'historically'. The themes of exile and return, sin and repentance, are demonstrated again and again in the Bible, from the Creation to the end of time. The theologian Rudolf Bultmann credits the notion that history has meaning and purpose to the Jews and Christians, whose understanding of history depended on eschatology:

> The Greeks did not raise the question of meaning in history and the ancient philosophers had not developed a philosophy of history. A philosophy of history grew up for the first time in Christian thinking, for Christians believed they knew of the end of the world and of history.

Bultmann concludes that the idea of historical progress that appears in the writings of the German philosopher G. W. F. Hegel and those of Karl Marx, is really a secularized version of Christian eschatology.

> Hegel and Marx, each in his own way, believed they knew the goal of history and interpreted the course of history in the light of this presupposed goal.

Jewish nationalism, or Zionism, actualizes the eschatological expectations surrounding the coming of the Messiah by de-supernaturalizing the Redeemer, placing the destiny of Israel in human hands. Most Jewish people regard themselves as descendants of the ancient Hebrew occupants of Palestine. Whether or not one regards such claims as sustainable in the face of contradictory historical and genetic evidence, the idea of Jewish ethnicity is underpinned by the religion, with Jewish identity predicated on a religious tradition extending back to antiquity. The Zionist movement secularized that tradition, without providing an unchallengeable notion of secular Jewishness.

Jewish ritual is centred on the myth of Exodus and the stories of the Jews in their ancient homeland. Before the Nazi Holocaust, however, the greeting 'Next Year in Jerusalem!' used by worshippers on High Holidays was usually understood symbolically or prophetically, as a hope to be deferred to the end of time. When political Zionists began transforming the messianic promise of redemption into a practical programme in the late 19th century, their religious leaders were appalled. The yearning for Zion, they argued, was a spiritual longing, to be assuaged only at the eschaton or end of days, when the Messiah would come and restore the land of Israel to its rightful owners. To turn this religious vision into a political reality was both foolish and blasphemous. Some orthodox rabbis went so far as to excommunicate the Zionists. However perilous the situation facing Jewish communities in Europe, especially those living under Russian rule, the Zionist solution was unacceptable. If the Zionists had their way, Jewish life would be directed away from religious observance and the study of holy texts, towards a political project outside the control of the rabbis.

Secular Zionism had a nationalist premiss: without a territory of their own, the Jews could not become a proper 'people' – like English, French, Germans, Greeks, Italians, Irish, Poles, or Czechs. The Zionist idea was predicated on the principle of national self-determination as famously articulated by U.S. President Wilson after the First World War. But Zionism also drew heavily on the eschatological ideas embedded in Jewish religious tradition. Redemption meant the physical return of Jews to the Land of Israel – a sacred territory promised to their Hebrew ancestor Abraham by God. Redemption conveys both secular and religious meanings. Irredentism – the urge to restore unredeemed land to the nation – was an important component of the nationalist movements, including fascism and Nazism, that emerged in Europe after the First World War. Non-religious Zionism shares with fascism the idea that a particular piece of territory belongs inalienably to one nation: in this respect, there is no essential difference in kind between Zionist claims on Palestine and, say, the Italian irredentist claims on the port of Fiume on the Dalmatian coast, a part of the formerly Venetian territory awarded to Yugoslavia after the First World War. Yet even the secular right-wing Zionists known as revisionists perceived Israel's expanding borders as stages on the road to redemption. Ian Lustick calls them, somewhat oxymoronically, the 'non-religious wing of the fundamentalist movement'. Led by Geula Cohen and Rafael Eitan, the revisionists see the religious Zionists' emphasis on the Land of Israel and its settlement as opportunity to enlist the support of religious Jews for maximalist nationalist aims. As Cohen explained: 'All members of Tehiya believe that we are living at the beginning of Redemption even if no one knows its exact definition.' By deliberately exploiting the eschatological expectations of the religious right, these secular right-wing Zionists acknowledge that religion is a more effective ideological basis for their expansionist aims than the strand of secular or romantic nationalism they themselves represent.

Similarly, the goal of *aliya*, the in-gathering of the Jews from all over the world, exemplified in Israel's Law of Return (which automatically confers citizenship on anyone who can prove his or her Jewish descent), is both secular and religiously eschatological in character. The boundaries between the secular nationalist ideology of 'redemption' and a religious one are inextricably blurred.

Gush Emunim, the principal settler movement, founded by members of the National Religious Party in 1974, explicitly describes its aim as being 'the redemption of the Land of Israel in our time'. This was to be achieved by allowing Jews to settle anywhere in the occupied territories, and by political campaigning. Gush Emunim members saw themselves as reviving ancient Israel. They named their settlements after ancient biblical towns and their children after Old Testament heroes. As their leader, Rabbi Moshe Levinger, put it, the land conquered in 1967 had been returned to its rightful owners as promised to their biblical ancestors by God. Gush Eminum deliberately breached Israeli government rules banning settlements near Arab towns. As one of their leaders, Rabbi Ben Nun, declared:

> Jewish immigration to Israel and settlement are beyond the law. The settlers' movement comes out of the Zionist constitution and no law can stop it. For those to whom the Bible and the religious prescripts are beyond the law there is no need to say anything further.

To the charge that they were acting in contravention to the will of the people expressed through their elected government, another Gush Emunim rabbi replied:

> For us, what really matters is not democracy, but the Kingdom of Israel. Democracy is a sacred idea for the Greeks, not so for the Jews.

Just as many Palestinians have come to admire the suicide bombers who have inflicted misery on Jewish families, the Israeli settlers have made heroes out of killers. Extremist rabbis commended

Baruch Goldstein, the American-educated physician who massacred at least 29 Muslim worshippers at the Tomb of the Patriarchs in Hebron in February 1994 before being killed by the crowd. For them, he is a 'holy martyr' who will act as the settlers' intercessor in heaven. Goldstein's status as martyr is the mirror-image of the Palestinian suicide bomber whose act of terror is described as an act of 'self-martyrdom' (*istishad*). In like fashion, the status of hero-martyrs has been conferred on Khalid Islambouli, executed for assassinating Anwar Sadat, the Egyptian president who signed the Camp David Peace Treaty with Israel, and Yigael Amir, assassin of Israeli Prime Minister Yitzhak Rabin, who signed the Oslo Accords with PLO Chairman Yasser Arafat. Amir, who has been described as a 'serious, deeply religious and well-adjusted student', made no secret of his view that Rabin was *din rodef* – the Halachic term for a traitor who endangers Jewish lives, and may therefore be killed as a measure of communal self-defence. Before he shot Rabin at point-blank range, he had ritually purified himself and obtained a rabbinical ruling in justification of his action. Islambouli's mentor, the engineer Abd al-Salaam al-Farraj, drew heavily on the writings of the medieval theologian Ibn Taymiyya, who condemned the Mongol rulers of Syria for failing to rule in accordance with Islamic law.

The religious Zionists of Gush Emunim who refuse to give back Arab territory, and the Islamists of Hamas and Islamic Jihad who refuse any accommodation with Israel, are in paradoxical collusion against secular-minded Jews and Palestinians in their opposition to any settlement involving a mutual accommodation between the contested territorial claims of Israel and Palestine. The old-style secular nationalists of the Palestine Liberation Organization (PLO) have met (in principle) the secular demands of Israel by accepting its right to exist as a Jewish state in accordance with United Nations resolutions. The Israelis, for their part, have given formal recognition to Palestinian rights by accepting the reality of the Palestine National Authority, while colluding with the settlers in limiting its power and undermining its authority. There exists a

8. Israeli premier Yitzhak Rabin, 1994

9. Yigael Amir, the assassin of Yitzhak Rabin, in court in Tel Aviv, 1995

precarious basis for an accommodation, but the religious
rejectionists on both sides are making this difficult, if not
impossible, by raising the ante, elevating the historic quarrel
between Arabs and Israelis into a Manichaean struggle between the
absolute values of good and evil. The prospects for peace are
further diminished by the support Christian fundamentalists have

10. Egyptian president Anwar al-Sadat

been lending to the US administration with its distinct pro-Israeli bias.

When conflicts are hyped in this way, violence is the inevitable concomitant. Religious nationalism further inflates nationalist rhetoric by giving it a cosmic dimension. For Hamas and other Islamist organizations, the struggle with Israel is transnational and cosmic. A communiqué issued after US troops were sent to Saudi Arabia in 1990 described it as another episode in the 'fight between good and evil and a hateful Christian plot against our religion, our civilization and our land'. In January 2003 President George W. Bush himself echoed the rhetoric of the Islamists like bin Laden who see conflicts between Muslim and Western governments in terms of an age-long struggle between good Muslims and evil Jews and Crusaders, when he packaged Arab nationalist Iraq, Islamist Iran, and communist North Korea – three countries with utterly different ideologies and with few, if any, connections between them – into a monolithic 'axis of evil' to be resisted by America.

The effect of such rhetoric is twofold. In societies such as America, Ireland, or parts of the Muslim world where religion has been an important part of the culture as well as an agent of socialization, the use of religious language has great mobilizing potential. People will respond positively to political messages couched in language associated with religion, because religion is thought of as good. But the use of such language also tends to transcendentalize disputes, elevating them, as it were, from the mundane to the cosmic level. The result is that conflicts are absolutized, rendering them more intractable, less susceptible to negotiation. Where people acknowledge the realities of competing interests (as, for example, in the national bargaining sessions over agricultural quotas in the European Union), compromise is not only possible: it is the only game in town. Where religious language is invoked, as in Ireland or Israel-Palestine, the play of interests is transcendentalized, subsumed, as it were, into a much grander, Manichaean contest, between polarized opposites of absolute good versus evil. Since every nationalist group is likely to clash with the competing nationalisms of its neighbours, religious language intensifies conflict, because most nationalisms arise where identities are contested or where land is subject to competing claims. The use of religious language as a strategy for mobilizing support is most likely to succeed in situations where national or ethnic identities are grounded in religion or sustained by religious differences. In absolutizing the conflict, the play of competing interests – the stuff of normal politics – is forgotten or overruled.

The Israeli example is instructive. As members of a First World, industrial society accustomed to Western lifestyles, with swimming pools, flush-toilets, and other modern conveniences, the Israeli settlers are greedy for water, a scarce resource in Palestine. According to recent estimates, Israeli settlers are now using 80% of the water available to farmers in Palestine. When religious language is used, the illegal and disproportionate use of water is translated into a God-given grant of land and water-rights to Abraham. In the biblical rhetoric of the settlers, the Jews are God's special people; the Arab Palestinians are identified with the Amalekites, a Canaanite tribe whom the ancient Hebrews were commanded to annihilate totally, with their women, children, and flocks. Where good and evil, God and the Devil, are ranged in opposite camps, who would deliberately choose the latter? Far from being its ideological competitor, the religious fundamentalism in Israel-Palestine, Chechnya, Kashmir, and many other of the world's most troubled regions is best understood as an intensification or deepening of nationalism by way of religion's catalysing force.

On the face of it, the three Abrahamic monotheisms might seem more susceptible to political exploitation of the kind we have been describing than Hindu polytheism or Buddhism, because of the absence in these traditions of an orthodoxy based on a single scriptural tradition. Hinduism is not so much a single religion as a loose collection of traditions (that of the Shaivites, the Vaishnavas, the Shaktas, the Smartas, and others) that share some common themes while tolerating a remarkable variety of religious expressions. Unlike the Abrahamic traditions, each of which has a canonical scripture that can function as a rallying point for defence, the Hindu tradition contains such an abundance of scriptures, laws, and philosophies that it becomes very difficult to single out any one specific item as being basic or 'fundamental'.

Nevertheless, there are some compelling parallels, or 'family resemblances', with the fundamentalisms one finds in the Abrahamic traditions. Like its Islamic counterpart, Hindu revivalism, with its nationalist or fundamentalist offshoots, is rooted in a reformist religious tradition more than a century old. The original movement was not in the first instance anti-Muslim but anti-colonial, stimulated by the British administration's pigeonholing of India's religious communities into identifiable and hence manageable groups. From the 1871 census the British defined their Indian subjects according to religion. With the introduction of democratic institutions at local level, starting in 1909, religious groupings were organized into separate electorates, with a number of constituencies reserved for Muslims in each province, and similar arrangements for Christians in Madras and Sikhs in the Punjab. For the educated Hindu elite, the need to cultivate their own constituencies meant delineating a broad-based communal identity beyond the old caste system. The creation of a new Hindu identity inevitably generated reciprocal responses amongst Muslims and Sikhs (as well as from the smaller Jain and Parsee communities whose separate identities were acknowledged), with all of the three main groups competing against each other for a privileged position in colonial society.

The reformist movements within Hinduism (a term invented by Europeans) bear some family resemblances to the Islamic *salafi* movement that originated in colonial Egypt towards the end of the 19th century. Swami Dayananda Sarasvati (1824–83), founder of Arya Samaj (the Society of Aryas), is one of the spiritual and intellectual progenitors of the RSS (Rashtriya Svayamsevak Sangh, or 'national union of volunteers') and its offshoot the BJP (Bharatiya Janata Party) – the senior partner in the coalition that governed India from 1998 to 2004). In some respects, he resembles Afghani in his rejection of tradition and the search he undertook for a modernized, more rational religion that would regenerate his society. A Brahman from a well-to-do Shaivite family in Gujarat, he was profoundly affected, aged 14, by watching a mouse consume (and pollute) offerings of food made to the statue of Shiva during an all-night vigil when other members of his family had dozed off. After wandering around India for 13 years as a holy man (a conventional apprenticeship for an aspiring guru), Dayananda found a teacher who persuaded him to preach his reformist doctrines in Hindi (the popular vernacular) rather than in learned Sanskrit.

Some of Dayananda's ideas reveal an affinity with the fundamentalisms to be found in the Abrahamic traditions. He believed that the Indian scriptures, the Vedas, were the highest revelations ever vouchsafed to humanity, and contained all knowledge, scientific as well as spiritual. All the knowledge that is extant in the world, he would claim, originated in Aryavarta, the Land of Arya, his name for ancient India, a mythical realm whose kings ruled over all the earth and taught wisdom to all their peoples. Through their vast knowledge, the ancient Indians were able to produce the weapons of war described in the great epics such as the *Mahabharata*. Since the knowledge of the Vedas is of general applicability, all references to kings and battles are in fact political or military directives. The sentiment is identical to that of the Islamists who recall the age of the Rightly Guided Caliphs as an era of justice and prosperity (although, in actual fact, three of the first four caliphs were brutally murdered). His point about military directives is strikingly similar to an argument employed by the Islamist writer Sayyid Qutb in *Milestones*, the tract he wrote while in prison in Egypt before his execution in 1966. Muhammad's Companions, according to Qutb, used the Koran not just for aesthetic or even moral guidance, but as a manual for action, as a soldier on the battlefield reads his daily bulletin.

Dayananda's ideas first took root among Hindus in the Punjab, which has large Muslim and Sikh populations, and it was Punjabi leaders of the Arya Samaj who founded the Punjab Hindu

Provincial Sabha (council), the first politically oriented Hindu group, in 1909. By 1921, it had become the All-India Hindu Mahasabha (great council), one of the best-known institutions of Hindu reaction. The council actively fostered the growth of the RSS. Now a highly professional organization with 25,000 branches throughout the country, the RSS has lent its organizational skills to two political parties, the Jana Sangh and its *de facto* successor, the BJP. Both L. K. Advani, president of the BJP, and the former Indian Prime Minister A. B. Vajpayee started their careers as RSS organizers.

The parallels with the Muslim Brotherhood founded in British-dominated Egypt in 1928, just three years after the RSS, are compelling. Both movements adopted something of the style of their colonial masters: the Muslim Brotherhood had affinities with the Boy Scout Movement and Young Men's Christian Association (YMCA) organizations that stressed the importance of physical activity, with paramilitary overtones. The khaki shorts worn by RSS volunteers during their drills were modelled on the uniform of the British Indian police. Both organizations discouraged democratic dissent under an authoritarian style of leadership. Both organizations encouraged male bonding by excluding women (though both allowed the creation of smaller all-female organizations). Both opposed the mixing of sexes within the organization as contrary to religious norms.

Like the Muslim Brothers, members of the RSS are organized into groups that transcend or substitute for family ties. Hasan al-Banna, founder of the Muslim Brotherhood, grouped his followers into families and battalions; young Palestinians who today volunteer for suicide missions are organized into friendship packs who may act as family substitutes, while holding them to their decision. The organizers of the RSS model themselves on Hindu renunciates. 'Dedicated to a higher goal [they] are supposed to abandon family ties and material wealth.' Like the Palestinian and Lebanese volunteers belonging to the Shia Hezbollah, they are generally young, unmarried men in their 20s. They wear Indian-style dress and are expected to lead an exemplary, ascetic existence, although some may marry and have families after a period of service. Organizers serve without salary, but their material needs are taken care of. Some volunteers are provided with motor scooters for getting around town. Both the Brotherhood and the RSS consciously blend elements of modernity with aspects of tradition, combining indigenous ideas of spiritual leadership with organizational techniques borrowed from Western bureaucracy.

The Hindu movement's leading intellectual was V. D. Savarkar (1883–1966), who held the presidency of the Hindu Mahasabha from 1937 to 1942. Like Sayyid Qutb, he wrote his most influential work, *Hindutva* ('Hindu-ness'), in prison, where he spent many years after his detention by the British in 1910. *Hindutva* is a manifesto for religious nationalism. As Daniel Gold explains, Savarkar's

> idea of Hindu Nation stands in contrast to the idea of a composite, territorially defined political entity that developed among the secular nationalists and would be enshrined in the Indian constitution. The modern western idea of nation, according to Savarkar, does not do justice to the ancient glory of the Hindu people, the indigenous and numerically dominant population of the subcontinent. The subcontinent is their motherland, and Hinduness is the quality of their national culture.

Hindutva is not the same as Hindu religious orthodoxy because, according to Savarkar, its spirit is manifest in other South Asian religions, including Jainism, Sikhism, and Indian Buddhism. Muslims and Christians, by contrast, are seen as foreign elements in the subcontinent, which rightly belongs to Hindus.

The RSS leader M.S. Golwalkar, like his Indian contemporary, the Islamist ideologue Mawdudi, expressed his admiration for the Nazis in Germany, who held similar ideas about national purity. 'Germany has shocked the world by purging the country of the semitic races the Jews', he wrote in 1939 – 'a good lesson for us in Hindusthan to learn and profit by'. As suggested above, there is a fundamentalistic element in Dayananda's elevation of the Vedas to the sum of human knowledge, along with his myth of the golden age of Aryavartic kings. But the predominant tone, and its consequences, are nationalist. *Hindutva* secularizes Hinduism by sacralizing the nation, bringing the cosmic whole within the realm of human organization. As Daniel Gold astutely observes:

> If personal religion entails among other things the identification of the individual with some larger whole, then the Hindu Nation may appear as a whole more immediately visible and attainable than the ritual cosmos of traditional Hinduism.

The problem, of course, is that such a sacralization of nationality is explicitly anti-pluralistic. Both Arya Samaj and the RSS define their religion in contradistinction to other groups. The Hinduization of Indian nationalism generated a reciprocal response among Muslims that led to the traumatic partition of the subcontinent in 1947, with many thousands killed or maimed in communal rioting. The shock of the sainted Mahatma Gandhi's assassination by an RSS member in January 1948 allowed Nehru to ban the RSS and its affiliates, enabling Congress to foist upon India a secular constitution that lies squarely in the best Western tradition. As Sunil Khilnani, one of India's foremost historians, has pointed out:

> Constitutional democracy based on universal suffrage did not emerge from popular pressures for it within Indian society, it was not wrested by the people from the state; it was given to them by the political choice of an intellectual elite.

The sacralization of Indian identity would remain a potent, corrosive force in the body politic, a sleeping giant that could all too easily be woken by politicians willing to play the communal card. Job reservations or affirmative action programmes aimed at protecting scheduled castes (the former Untouchables), could be presented as clashing with the rights or aspirations of the majority. In the words of a former state director-general of police and official of the VHP affiliated to the RSS: 'We feel that what we are doing is good for the country. After all what is good for 82% of the country is good for the rest of the country, isn't it?' The 'Fundamental Rights' guaranteeing 'freedom of conscience and free profession, practice and propagation or religion' under article 25 of the constitution would remain highly problematic in a society as religious as India's. As T. N. Madan points out:

> secularism does not mean in India that religion is privatized: such an idea is alien to the indigenous religious traditions, which are holistic in character and do not recognize such dualistic categories as sacred versus profane, religious versus secular, or public versus private.

One of the severest tests facing India's secular constitutional arrangements has come from the fundamentalist, or rather religious nationalist, movement within the minority Sikh community. The militant Sikh movement led by the charismatic preacher Jarnail Singh Bhindranwale (1947–84) fits the pattern of movements in other religious traditions that have turned to, or ended in, violence. A relatively young religion founded in the Punjab during the 16th century, Sikhism constantly faced the possibility of being reabsorbed into the Hindu mainstream from which it originally sprang. Like other fundamentalist leaders, Bhindranwale strongly resisted the pressures towards assimilation, whether Hinduistic or secular Western. In his preaching he called for a return to the original teachings of the ten gurus and strict adherence to their codes of moral conduct, paying more attention to politics and social behaviour than to the cosmological questions the religion addresses.

In defending his community against the perceived cultural encroachments of Hindu Punjabis, Bhindranwale unleashed a campaign of terror that cost hundreds of innocent Hindu lives. To the symbolic or latent militancy of Sikhism represented by beard, dagger, and sword he added two new items: the revolver and the motorcycle. Towards the end of 1983, fearing arrest, Bhindranwale and dozens of armed supporters installed themselves in the compound surrounding the Golden Temple at Amritsar, the holiest shrine of Sikhism, an area constantly thronged with visitors, pilgrims, priests, and auxiliary helpers. By taking refuge in the temple area, he challenged the government to defile the sanctuary using the pilgrims and others as human shields, while permitting his followers to desecrate it.

There are parallels here with the seizure of the sanctuary in Mecca, Islam's holiest shrine, by the Saudi rebel Juhaiman al-Utaibi in

11. **Bhindranwale (pointing) confronts Sikh guards at the Golden Temple**

November 1979. Operation Blue Star, the Indian Army's attack on the Golden Temple in June 1984, resulted in more than a thousand deaths (including Bhindranwale's), many of them innocent pilgrims. Shortly afterwards, Prime Minister Indira Gandhi, who authorized the attack, was murdered by her trusted Sikh bodyguards. Nearly 3,000 Sikhs lost their lives in the ensuing rioting in Delhi and other cities. In a retaliatory attack, Sikh terrorists may have been responsible for the crash of an Air India jumbo jet off the Irish coast in June 1985, killing all 329 people on board.

The second major challenge to India's secular constitution took place seven years later, in 1992, when a gang of Hindu militants destroyed the Babri Masjid (mosque of Babur) in the town of Ayodhya, southeast of Delhi. Ayodhya is the mythical birthplace of Lord Rama, hero of the *Rayama*, one of the great Indian epics, and an incarnation of the great god Vishnu. The Kingdom of Ayodhya, over which Rama rules with his beautiful consort Sita after his exile and travails in the forest, epitomizes the golden age of Aryavarta as described by Dayananda. Rama's alleged birthplace, however, became the site of a mosque said to have been constructed on the orders of Babur, the first Moghul emperor, after a visit to the city in 1528. In 1949, two years after Independence, local worshippers reported the miraculous appearance of Rama's image in the building. (Muslims, more sceptically, believed it had been put there by local Hindu activists.) An outbreak of communal rioting persuaded the local magistrate to close the building, but he allowed Hindu worshippers to visit it once a year on the anniversary of the image's appearance. The build-up to the crisis started in earnest in 1986 when a local court allowed the building to be opened for Hindu worship. In the ensuing riots, bombs were set off, shops were burned, and at least 20 people died. By 1989, the confrontation had became a major national issue, with an all-India campaign by Hindu activists to construct a new temple at the site. Small donations were sought from millions of ordinary people; villagers from all over India collaborated in making bricks for the temple's

12. Indira Gandhi

construction. Tensions escalated throughout the summer, with increasing communal rioting taking place as the elections approached. The government's efforts at mediation were unsuccessful, and in November the Congress faction led by Indira's son Rajiv Gandhi was defeated at the polls. His successor proved no more successful at defusing the tension. In December 1992, in defiance of the courts and their own religious leaders, Hindu militants demolished the mosque during a ceremony for the dedication of the new temple, many of them using their bare hands.

In an action that infuriated India's Muslims (and would have wide repercussions in Pakistan), the 19,000 police and militiamen who had been drafted to protect the site failed to intervene. The subsequent riots in Bombay and other cities were the worst since India's independence in 1947. In a series of pogroms, thousands of

13. **Destruction of the Babri Masjid, Ayodhya, India, December 1992**

innocent Muslims lost their lives: even in Bombay's affluent Colobar district, where real estate prices rival those of Tokyo and New York, middle-class Muslims found it necessary to remove their names from lists of residents on apartment blocks, fearing lynching by the mob.

Sri Lanka provides a further example of South Asian religious nationalism. Here, in a situation that bears a certain resemblance to Ireland, the demand for recognition of its separate status by an island minority linked by religion and ethnicity to its larger neighbour (in this case Hindu Tamils of southern India) is perceived by members of the majority community Sinhalese Buddhists as a threat to the nation's integrity. Like Irish Catholicism, the Theravada Buddhism of Sri Lanka has developed into a nationalist ideology in which religion has become a marker of communal identity. The reasons are largely historical. Sri Lankan Buddhists regard themselves as the survivors of the great Buddhist empire founded in India by King Asoka in the 3rd century BCE. While in mainland India Buddhism eventually disappeared as society relapsed into the multiform patterns of worship which came to be known as Hinduism, the Sinhalese held to the Buddhist faith, which eventually became politicized. In Sri Lanka (according to Donal Swearer), Buddhism provided the stirrings of anti-colonial sentiment by offering 'the only universally acceptable symbol to represent an accumulation of grievances – economic, social, and psychological – which were as yet, for the most part, inarticulate and incapable of direct political exploitation.'

A reformist movement among the laity, stimulated in part by the American theosophist Colonel Olcott, won some concessions from the British, but in general the colonial authorities were hostile towards the Buddhist *sangha* (religious institution), which they saw as a threat to their power. The most articulate spokesman of the new reformed or nationalist Buddhism came to be known as the Anagarika Dharmapala (the 'Homeless Guardian' of the Dharma or universal law). An Afghani-like figure who occupied a position somewhere between a monk and a lay politician, he formulated, according to Donald Swearer, a simplified, moralistic Buddhist ideology that was doubtless stimulated by the challenge posed by Protestant missionaries. Like Hasan al-Banna, Dharmapala fulminated against the social vices deemed to have been introduced under colonial auspices, while harking back to an early, heroic age when righteousness prevailed – in this case, the reign of King Dutthagamani (161–137 BCE), who wrested control from a Tamil ruler and thus became an exemplary nationalist hero:

> My message to the young men of Sri Lanka is Believe not the alien who is giving you arrack, whisky, toddy, sausages, who makes you buy his goods at clearance sales. Enter into the realm of our King Dutthagamani in spirit and try to identify yourself with the thoughts of the great king who rescued Buddhism and our nationalism from oblivion.

In 1956, the year of Britain's Suez debacle, S. W. R. D. Bandaranaike, leader of the opposition Sri Lankan Freedom Party (SLFP), was able to win power on a pro-Buddhist, pro-Sinhalese ticket, replacing the upper-class, English-educated liberals of the United National Party who had governed the country since independence. The SLFP benefited hugely from celebration of the 2,500th anniversary of the Buddha's birth (Buddha Jayanti) the following year and from the previous publication of a report detailing the suppression of Buddhism under the British. The Jayanti enlarged upon and celebrated the national myth bonding the Buddhist faith to the land and the Sinhalese nation which had 'come into being with the blessing of the Buddha as a "chosen race" with a divine mission to fulfil, and now stands on the threshold of a new era leading to its "great destiny"'. The SLFP was aggressively supported by the United Monks' Front, which rejected the concept of secular nationhood in terms very similar to those that would be used by the Iranian leader Ayatollah Khomeini in his famous Najaf lectures.

The 'Buddhisization' of Sri Lankan politics had the inevitable consequence of making non-Buddhists (Tamils and Muslims) feel excluded from the nation, provoking demands by Tamil separatists for a state of their own.

> In ancient days, according to the records of history, the welfare of the nation and the welfare of the religion were regarded as synonymous terms by the laity as well as by the Sangha. The divorce of religion from the nation was an idea introduced into the minds of the Sinhalese by invaders from the West who belonged to an alien faith. It was a convenient instrument of astute policy to enable them to keep the people in subjugation in order to rule the people as they pleased. It was in their own interests and not for the welfare of the people that these foreign invaders attempted to create a gulf between the bhikkus (monks) and the laity – a policy which they implemented with diplomatic cunning. We should not follow their example and should not attempt to withdraw the bhikkus from society. Such conduct would assuredly be a deplorable act of injustice, committed against our nation, our country, our religion.
>
> (Statement by the United Monks' Front, 1946, in Donald K. Swearer, 'Fundamentalist Movements in Theravada Buddhism', in Marty and Appleby, *Fundamentalism Observed*)

The Tamil Tigers, as the activists called themselves, were concerned not only with securing political rights, but more importantly with maintaining a cultural, ethnic, and religious identity which had been suppressed or alienated as Sinhalese nationalism became increasingly reliant on Buddhist symbols. More than 60,000 people from both communities lost their lives in the ensuing civil war that lasted nearly two decades. In the late 1980s, the Tigers resorted increasingly to the novel tactic – pioneered by the Shii Hezbollah in Lebanon – of suicide bombing. More often than not the victims were civilians. A steady campaign of assassinations (including that of the Indian prime minister, Rajiv Gandhi, in 1991, by a female bomber) and indiscriminate murder was kept up through the 1990s and lasted well into the 2000s.

The example of Buddhism in Sri Lanka clearly demonstrates that none of the major religious traditions is immune from fundamentalism, to which violence is closely linked, though it might be better in this, as in most other contexts, to describe the process as the 'nationalization' or secularization of religion. Donald Swearer argues that by homogenizing the Buddhist tradition and reducing it to a simplified core teaching along with a moralistic programme of right living linked to Sinhalese Buddhist identity, Bandaranaike (and his later successor President Jayawardine) 'ignored the polar dynamic between the transmundane and the mundane, a distinction basic not only to traditional Theravada Buddhism but to the other great historical religions as well. The absolutism of fundamentalism', he concludes, 'stems from this basic transformation of the religious worldview.' It is not religious in the classical sense of that term but rather a variant of a secular faith couched in religious language, in which 'religious symbols are stripped of their symbolic power to evoke a multiplicity of meanings'.

The heart of the fundamentalist project, in line with this analysis, lies not in religion itself but in the essentially modern agenda of extending or consolidating the power of the national state or, to use the term preferred by the Israeli sociologist S. N. Eisenstadt, the revolutionary 'Jacobin' state that appeared with the French Revolution and the movements that surfaced in its wake, including communism and fascism. According to Eisenstadt, the fundamentalists appropriated some of the 'central aspects of the political program of modernity', including its 'participatory, totalistic, and egalitarian orientations' while rejecting the

Enlightenment values embedded in Jacobinism, including the sovereignty and autonomy of reason and the perfectibility of man. 'The basic structure or phenomenology of their vision and action', he concludes,

> is in many crucial and seemingly paradoxical ways a modern one, just as was the case with the totalitarian movements of the twenties and thirties. These movements bear within themselves the seeds of very intensive and virulent revolutionary sectarian, utopian Jacobinism, seeds which can, under appropriate circumstances, come to full-blown fruition.

Such movements have always had violent repercussions: before developing its modern meaning of freelance or irregular military action, the word 'terrorist' was applied to the Jacobin revolutionaries in France who used the power of the state to inflict terror on their enemies.

A common feature of all such movements may be found in the way that religion has become secularized in many parts of the world, even among people who claim to be resisting secularism. The mythical images of cosmic struggle that form part of the religious repertoire of the great traditions are being actualized or brought down to earth. The cosmic struggle is understood to be occurring in this world rather than in a mythical setting. Believers identify personally with the struggle. All religions affirm the primacy of meaning and order over chaos; hence in treating of death and violence, religions strive to contain them within an overarching, benign cosmic frame. In the Baghavad Gita, the god Krishna tells the warrior Arjuna that he must submit to his destiny in fighting against his own kinsmen. In so doing, he assents to the disorder of the world, although the contestants know that in the grander sense, this disorder is corrected by a cosmic order that is beyond killing and being killed. Similarly, the Koran contains many allusions to the Prophet Muhammad's battles, which are set in the wider context of a moral order deemed to be upheld by an all-seeing benevolent God. For Christians, Jesus's heroism in allowing himself to endure an excruciatingly painful death is seen as a monumental act of redemption for humankind, tipping the balance of power and allowing the struggle for order to succeed.

Religious images and texts provide ways in which violence, pain, and death are overcome symbolically. Human suffering is made more durable by the idea that death and pain are not pointless, that lives are not wasted needlessly, but are part of a grander scheme in which divinely constituted order reigns supreme above the chaos and disorder of the world. In such a context, the horrors and chaos of wars, as described in the Mahabharata and the Book of Joshua, as debated in the Baghavad Gita, as predicted in the Book of Revelation, and as alluded to in the Koran, are subsumed within an order seen to be meaningful and ultimately benign. The reading and recitation of such texts over the centuries, like the performance of ancient Greek tragedies, doubtless had a carthartic function, purging people of anger and rage, inducing pity and fear, reducing actual conflict, upholding social harmony. By its rejection of symbolic interpretations fundamentalism (at least in its politically militant versions) releases the violence contained in the text. Fundamentalism is religion materialized, the word made flesh, as it were, with the flesh rendered, all too often, into shattered body parts by the forces of holy rage.

Why is this happening in the 21st century? Why, when modernization seemed to have made the God of Battles redundant, if not dead, has religious violence resurfaced, like Dracula, from the grave?

Chapter 7
Conclusion

> The rise of urban civilization and the collapse of traditional religion are the two main hallmarks of our era and are closely related movements . . . What is secularization? . . . It is the loosening of the world from religion and quasi-religious understandings of itself . . . The gods of traditional religions live on as private fetishes or the patrons of congenial groups, but they play no role whatever in the public life of the secular metropolis . . . It will do no good to cling to our religions and metaphysical version of Christianity in the hope that one day religion or metaphysics will once again be back. They are disappearing *forever* [emphasis added] and that means we can now let go and immerse ourselves in the new world of the secular city.
>
> (Harvey Cox, *The Secular City*, 1965)

Until the mid-1970s, it was widely assumed that politics was breaking away from religion and that as societies became more industrialized, religious belief and practice would be restricted to private thoughts and activities. The decline in the social and political importance of religion in the West was grounded in the social scientific traditions flowing from the commanding figures of

Karl Marx, Émile Durkheim, and Max Weber, all of whom insisted in different ways that secularization was integral to modernization. The processes of modern industrialism which Weber saw as being characterized by depersonalized functional relationships and increasing bureaucratization were leading, if not to the final death of God, at the least to the 'disenchantment of the world'. The numinous forces that had underpinned the medieval cosmos would be psychologized, subjectivized, and demythologized.

On the face of it, the 1979 revolution in Iran seriously dented conventional wisdom. Here was a revolt deploying a repertoire of religious symbols that brought down a modernizing government and placed political power in the hands of a religious establishment steeped in medieval theology and jurisprudence. Moreover, this was clearly an urban, not a rural, phenomenon – a response, perhaps, to over-rapid or uneven development, but not in any sense a movement such as the counter-revolutionary movements in the Vendée or the peasant jacqueries that challenged the secular project of the French Revolution.

By the early 1980s, however, it was becoming clear that religious activism was very far from being confined to the Islamic world and that newly politicized movements were occurring in virtually every major religious tradition. In America, the New Christian Right (NCR) challenged and temporarily checked the boundaries of church–state separation that had steadily been moving in a secular direction. The collapse of communism in Eastern Europe has seen a marked resurgence in public religiosity, while Latin America and parts of Africa appear to be undergoing far-reaching religious transformations, with Pentecostalism overtaking Catholicism as the dominant religious tradition. With Japan and South Korea – Asia's most advanced industrial economies – ranking high in the list of countries nurturing new religious movements, only secular Western Europe and Australasia, areas that Martin Marty, the American historian of religion, calls the 'spiritual ice-belt', appear to be conforming to the demise of the public deity so confidently predicted by the founding fathers of modern social science.

Various theories have been advanced to explain the persistence or recent revival of religion, of which the fundamentalisms we have been examining are an integral part. The two previous chapters explored the close connections between religious revival movements and nationalism. Where religion or in certain cases religious difference is a vital component in the construction of national identity or where religious feelings have been invoked in the course of the struggle against colonialism, as in many Third World countries, religious rhetoric retains its ability to mobilize and motivate. Thus, without abandoning the secularization thesis altogether, Jeff Haynes suggests that secularization continues to make 'sustained progress' except when religion finds or retains work to do other than its pre-modern function of 'relating individuals to the supernatural'. Haynes relates this paradoxically to the postmodern rejection of metanarratives or absolute ways of speaking truth.

> 'Postmodernism' is an enigmatic concept, whose very ambiguity reflects the confusion and uncertainty inherent in contemporary life. The term is applied in and to many diverse spheres of human life and activity. It is important for politics as it decisively reflects the end of belief in the Enlightenment project, the assumption of universal progress based on reason, and in the modern Promethean myth of humanity's mastery of its destiny and capacity for resolution of all its problems.

The relationship between fundamentalism and postmodernism is paradoxical because far from rejecting absolute ways of speaking truth, fundamentalisms exemplify them. The compliment postmodernism pays to religion is back-handed and treacherous. By proclaiming the end of positivism and the ideology of progress, which was supposed to have replaced or overtaken religion, postmodernism opens up public space for religion, but at the price of relativizing its claims to absolute truth. By saying, in effect, 'your story is as good as mine, or his, or hers', postmodernism allows religious voices to have their say while denying their right to silence others, as religions have tended to do throughout history. For the true fundamentalist, the 'post-' prefixed to modernism is a catch, perhaps even a fraud, because modernity, in Anthony Gidden's formulation, is founded on the institutionalization of doubt. Far from de-institutionalizing doubt, however, the pluralism implicit in a postmodernist outlook sanctifies it by opening the doors of choice, which is the enemy of certainty.

Theologically, fundamentalists must reject choice because they know there is only one truth that has been revealed to them by the supraempirical spiritual entity most of them call God. But the contemporary situation under which this deity (or in some cases deities) makes demands on them are utterly different from those that prevailed in pre-modern times, when most people were exposed to a single religious tradition within a cultural milieu largely formed by that tradition. The situation facing Muslims living in the West illustrates dilemmas that can be applied, with suitable modifications, to believers in other faith traditions who may feel ghettoized, or to those living as minorities in a globalized, predominantly secular culture conditioned by technologies originating in the post-Enlightenment West. For example, the formalistic dos and don'ts of Islam as contained in a popular compendium published by the fundamentalist Sheikh Yusuf al-Qaradawi reveals the skeleton of Islamically correct behaviour without showing the flesh-and-blood context in which the Islamic system of values used to operate. In a pluralistic world where Muslims are obliged to live cheek-by-jowl with non-Muslim neighbours, where almost everyone has access to televised images of what used to be called the domain of war or unbelief (*dar al-harb* or *dar al-kufr*), the modalities of everyday living acquire a significance they did not have before.

Under modern conditions, an open question – 'what is the proper way to behave?' – is replaced by a much narrower one: 'how should Muslims (or followers of other faith traditions) behave under modern conditions?', the implication being that for Muslims nowadays the whole world has become *dar al-harb* because, even in Muslim majority areas, ways of living differently from the straight path prescribed by Islam are ever-present alternatives. In pre-colonial times, during the era of what might be called the 'classical Islamic hegemony', the possibility of alternative non-Islamic lifestyles simply did not arise for the majority of people. Where pork is not available, no one has to make a decision about whether to eat hot-dogs. Where wine was the preserve of a privileged elite who drank it in the privacy of their palaces, the permissibility of alcohol consumption was not a burning social question. In a homosocial society where women were strictly segregated, lesbian and gay relationships (though formally prohibited) were rarely seen as threatening to the social order. Under pressures from outside forces, all these issues, especially those involving sexual appearance and behaviour, have acquired iconic significance as marking boundaries between the 'insiders' and 'outsiders', the 'community of salvation' and the 'unsaved' people who live beyond its boundaries. Thus, in an archetypically Western milieu such as the American high school, Muslim identity defaults to gender segregation, with veiled Muslim coeds holding all-female proms in order to avoid breaking the taboo on sexual mixing. Their evangelical Christian counterparts hold assemblies of promise-keepers, who proclaim their commitment to chastity before marriage and fidelity afterwards. In a pluralistic environment such as America, all religious groups will use behavioural restrictions as a way of marking the boundaries between believers and non-believers, between us (the saved) and them (the damned). Mormons abstain from tea and coffee as well as alcohol, so they are distinguishable from orthodox evangelicals, who are mostly teetotal. Jehova's Witnesses avoid blood transfusions (and military service), Christian Scientists avoid conventional medicine (because Christ is the only Healer), and some Hasidic Jews (like some ultra-orthodox Muslims) exhibit behaviour bordering on incivility by refusing to shake hands with non-believers. Such behaviour is often described by those whom it is designed to exclude as 'fundamentalist'. One of the family resemblances exhibited by movements in this book is the concern or even obsession with the drawing of boundaries that will set the group apart from the wider society by deliberately choosing beliefs or modes of behaviour which proclaim who they are and how they would like to be seen.

In this respect, fundamentalisms are distinctly modern phenomena: like the New Religious Movements that have sprouted in some of the most industrialized parts of the world (notably South East Asia and North America), they feed on contemporary alienation or anomie by offering solutions to contemporary dilemmas, buttressing the loss of identities sustained by many people (especially young people) at times of rapid social change, high social and geographic mobility, and other stress-inducing factors. As two well-known American observers, Anson Sharpe and Jeffrey Hadden, put it:

> Fundamentalism is a truly modern phenomenon: modern in the sense that the movement is always seeking original solutions to new, pressing problems. Leaders are not merely constructing more rigid orthodoxies in the name of defending old mythical orthodoxies. In the process of undertaking restoration within contemporary demographic/technological centres, *new* social orders are actually being promulgated.

The born-again Christian finds comfort and support, not just by internalizing the iconic figure of Jesus as a personal super-ego, but also by accessing the support of fellow believers. Islamist organizations such as Hamas are not just involved in armed resistance to the Israeli occupation of their land but dispose of a considerable range of welfare activities. As well as being places of worship, churches, mosques, and synagogues are the hubs of social networks. The intensive religiosity exhibited by fundamentalists in all traditions may strengthen the support and increase the social opportunities the individual receives from such networks, though there are perils here as well: in the absence of disciplined hierarchies, disputes about the interpretation of texts makes fundamentalists vulnerable to the splits that afflict most radical movements.

Many fundamentalisms differ from cults or New Religious Movements by their commitment to textual scripturalism. For example, the focus of the Rajneesh community in Oregon and Pune was on the person of Baghwan Shree Rajneesh, a charismatic cult leader who drew eclectically on a wide variety of sources from Hinduism, Buddhism, Christian and Islamic mysticism, psychoanalysis, and psychotherapy, as well as personal spiritual experience, in his teachings. A Christian fundamentalist such as Jerry Falwell, by contrast, sticks closely to the inerrant text of the Bible in his sermons. This distinction, however, should not be drawn too sharply. David Koresh, the prophet of the Branch Davidian sect of Seventh Day Adventism who perished along with dozens of his followers at Waco, Texas, in April 1993, when his compound was attacked by US federal agents, was a textual fundamentalist as well as a charismatic leader who availed himself of the sexual services of his female followers in order to 'spread his seed'. Far from being the result of brain-washing or mind-control techniques, the charismatic power he exercised over his followers was the result of their conviction that he was a divinely inspired interpreter of biblical passages (particularly the Book of Revelation) that are central to the Seventh Day Adventist tradition. During the prolonged negotiations preceding the federal attack on the Waco compound after a 51-day siege, the FBI negotiators dismissed Koresh's sermonizing as mere 'Bible babble'. To his followers, however, his discourses on the Christian apocalypse were both meaningful and pregnant with religious insight.

As these and many other examples suggest, it is not just religious movements designated as fundamentalist which have come to challenge the secularization thesis so confidently proclaimed by

14. Storming the Branch Davidian compound, Waco, Texas, 1982

Harvey Cox in the 1960s when he was Professor of Divinity at
Harvard. According to Anson Shupe and Jeffrey Hadden, the forces
of secularization, rather than being unidirectional, are part of a
dialectical process: 'the economic and secular forces of so-called
modernization contain the very seeds of a reaction that brings
religion back into the heart of concerns about public policy'. There
is an abundance of evidence to support this view in North America,
where the New Christian Right is actively engaged in Republican
politics. The same dialectical logic, however, also limits the
potential of fundamentalists to transform society in the direction
they want. As already noted, in order to maximize their electoral
appeal, fundamentalists in a democracy must compartmentalize
their theology and form alliances with other conservative religious
groups such as Mormons, Catholics, and conservative Jews whom
they must perforce regard as infidels. This not only dilutes the

religious aspect of the message, which is to convert non-believers; the very act of compartmentalization, of separating the religious from the political, undermines the fundamentalist agenda of bringing back God into politics.

A similar logic applies to television, the most conspicuous of the technologies used by fundamentalists in America. By means of television, 'televangelists' such as Pat Robertson seek to challenge the secular order, by re-enchanting the world with divine interventions and supernatural events. Robertson and the late Oral Roberts have performed healings on camera, even claiming to heal viewers through their sets. In such programmes the sacred is reaffirmed, after being banished from secular networks, or at best restricted to the realm of fiction. The process of modernization described by Weber in his famous phrase 'the disenchantment of the world' is reversed. Through television, the world is re-enchanted and resacralized.

At the same time, the counter-attack on secular values mounted through religious television may prove subject to the law of diminishing returns. Through television the sacred and supernatural are domesticated, and ultimately banalized. In the end, disenchantment continues under the guise of the new religiosity. In the studio the charismatic leader who speaks for God must put himself under the control of the director and camera crew. Sacred words may be lost in cyberspace or disappear on the cutting-room floor. The structure of authority becomes ambiguous.

Television, mixing fact and fiction within a common format, collapses *mythos* and *logos*, especially in cultures where the conventions of theatre and fiction have recently been imported. In India, movie stars who played divine beings in religious epics have turned themselves into politicians. The Ayodhya agitation referred to in Chapter 6 was boosted by television showings of the Ramayana; in the communal rioting that followed, Hindu and

Muslim agitators stirred up mutual hostility by showing videos of their co-religionists under attack.

In the *700 Club*, the supernatural is not just appropriated: it is routinized and domesticated, formatted into regular 15- to 20-minute slots. In normal parlance, a supernatural event is by definition unpredictable and awe-inspiring, since natural laws have been suspended or superseded. Yet on the *700 Club*, healings and other supernatural interventions, in which the divine is presumed to have acted on matter by the invocation of the Holy Spirit through prayer, occur so frequently as to be almost banal. In the community of the saved, as exhibited on CBN, God routinely suspends natural laws and processes. The miraculous is thus not so much a manifestation of the inexplicable Power of the Almighty, as the ritual confirmation of a belief-system that challenges the conventions of secular medical science. Like the Bible itself, the miraculous acts as a shibboleth or totem, reinforcing the identity of the group.

The increase in religious militancy, occurring in many traditions in defiance of the secularization thesis, may be related to the increasing power and accessibility of audiovisual media, but the long-term consequences are ambiguous. In the first instance, the fundamentalist impulse in many traditions has been a reaction to the invasive quality of film and television, which exposes sacred areas like sexual relations to public gaze, bringing transgressive images into the home. During the Islamist campaign in Algeria, technicians had their throats slit for fitting satellite dishes that would bring into Muslim homes images of the Satanic West, including semi-pornographic material from Italy and the Netherlands, as well as factual news channels. In America televangelists such as Falwell and Robertson fought back against the perceived secularization of the culture by creating their own religious programmes and television networks.

With the development of satellite networks such as the al-Jazeera

15. Jerry Falwell

channel based in Qatar, state-funded broadcasting monopolies are losing their ability to impose censorship and control information. In the least-developed regions, even more radical forces for change are at work, as the audiovisual revolution undercuts the authority of the literate elites. Societies such as Iran and India where levels of literacy have been low have moved from the oral to the audiovisual era without experiencing the revolution in literacy that generated both Protestantism and the Enlightenment in Europe.

Clearly, the revolution in communications has a bearing on the failure of the secularization thesis as promulgated by Cox and others. Where levels of literacy are low, the audio and video cassette have enabled charismatic religious figures such as Sheikh Qaradawi on al-Jazeera and the late Ayatollah Khomeini to acquire massive followings. Osama bin Laden's carefully crafted videos disseminated by al-Jazeera have contributed to his image as the archetypical Islamic hero. Audiovisual technologies restore the power of word and gesture, the traditional province of religion, to a new type of leader, undercutting the hegemony of bureaucrats and the traditional religious professionals whose source of information and power was the written word. When relayed on tape or television, the power of orality and the languages of ritual and gesture retain their potency.

Fundamentalisms have benefited from the revolution in communications in two ways. First, radio broadcasts and television images, which are now accessible to the majority of people on this planet, make people much more aware of issues with which they can identify than was the case in the past. They increase the political temperature and add to perceptions of cultural conflict. An obvious example is the Israeli-Palestinian conflict. Viewers throughout the Muslim world are enraged by the sight of Israeli soldiers killing and humiliating Palestinians, while viewers in the West, shocked and dismayed by the carnage inflicted by suicide bombers, are liable to have anti-Arab or anti-Muslim prejudices confirmed.

16. The remains of an Israeli bus after a suicide bombing

As numerous media theorists have pointed out, television is not the same as propaganda. It does not have a unidirectional or homogenizing impact on viewers. Most viewers bring pre-existing knowledge to what they see and hear on television, decoding images according to their prejudices. In the Muslim world, images of Israeli oppression may be reinforced by perceived differences in lifestyles. For example, the explicit sexual interactions to be seen on a Tel Aviv beach may add to Islamist perceptions that Palestinians are facing not just a racist enemy that discriminates against them, but one that is wholly evil because of its pagan (*jahili*) social attitudes. Secondly, as explained already, fundamentalists benefit from the para-personal, electronically amplified relationships between charismatic leaders and their audiences. Nasser and Hitler were both beneficiaries of the new medium of radio; both Khomeini and bin Laden seem to be iconically impressive figures able to convey the solemnity, gravitas, nobility, and asceticism Muslims associate with the aniconic image of the Prophet Muhammad.

But if fundamentalist movements benefit from the media revolution, they are also liable to be among its casualties. The development of satellite television and increasing access to the internet is bringing an end to the information monopolies on which fundamentalists, like other authoritarian movements, depend. In certain contexts, such as Israel-Palestine and Iraq after the Anglo-American invasion, armed resistance to an externally imposed authority, publicized by the media, is regarded as legitimate by a significant number of people. Under such circumstances (which usually fit the category of religious nationalism, rather than pure fundamentalism), the terrorists or martyrs may become heroes. But where religious radicals have tried to impose their will by violence, as in Egypt, the publicity they court by indulging in the propaganda of the deed may result in popular revulsion, especially in the pious middle-class constituencies on which they depend for support.

Where Islamists have succeeded in taking power, as in Iran, satellite technology tells against them, since it becomes impossible for them to sustain their monopoly over the religious discourse. Sacred texts such as the Koran have endured because they transcend ideologies, speaking to the human condition in language that is always open to alternative interpretations.

The future is nonetheless precarious. Soon two Islamist regimes, Iran and Pakistan, could be armed with nuclear weapons, a prospect made more dangerous by the strand of apocalyptic fantasy that excites and inspires the children of Abraham. In Israel-Palestine, following the triumph of Hamas in the elections to the Palestinian National Authority, Islamists are challenging not only the Israeli occupation, but the authority of the Palestinian leaders who signed the Oslo Accords with the Jewish state in 1993. Within three years, at this writing, an Iranian regime with nuclear capacity could be supporting the Palestinians in the next round of the *intifada* against Israel. Since the latter already has its nuclear weapons, the stage will be set for the Armageddon predicted and welcomed by premilliennialists as the necessary prelude to the return of Christ. The gloomy prognosis might be applied, *a fortiori*, to Pakistan, an economic and social disaster zone when compared with its rival, the polytheist or pagan India. More ominously even than in Israel-Palestine, the apocalyptic mood in Pakistan centres on the Islamic bomb, to which there are now flower-decked shrines in major cities. Like the attacks on New York and Washington, which like other cities in the Satanic West face the prospect of terrorist attacks with dirty bombs (conventional explosives containing radioactive materials capable of spreading radiation over a large area), Pakistani bomb-worship may be a manifestation of nihilistic theological despair. Polytheist India flourishes compared with rightly-guided Pakistan. So do infidel countries like South Korea and Japan. Since the God of Manifest Success who rewarded Muhammad on the field of battle has so signally failed to deliver, we must kill ourselves, taking with us as many of our enemies as we can.

The attacks of 9/11 revealed the dangers of this apocalyptic outlook. The leaders were not ignorant young men from a deprived region of the world protesting against economic injustices, but privileged enragés who could have expected to achieve high-status jobs in fields like medicine, engineering, and architecture. Their rage was theological: the God of Battles who looms so largely in the Abrahamic imagination had let them down disastrously. Their faith in the benign and compassionate deity of Islam had begun to wobble. Their final act was not a gesture of Islamic heroism, but of Nietzschean despair. The same mentality exists in the Western branch of what is often called 'fundamentalism' but might be better described as 'Abrahamic apocalypticism'. Christian premillennialists are theological refugees in a world they no longer control. In America, fortunately, their avenues of expression usually fall short of violence (though there have been physical attacks by fundamentalists on doctors performing abortions). However they have a baleful influence on American foreign policy, by tilting it towards the Jewish state, which they aim eventually to obliterate by converting righteous Jews to Christ. They have damaged the education of American children in some places by adding scientific creationism, or its successor 'intelligent design', to the curriculum.

They inconvenience some women especially poor women with limited access to travel by making abortion illegal in certain states. On a planetary level, they are selfish, greedy, and stupid, damaging the environment by the excessive use of energy and lobbying against environmental controls. What is the point of saving the planet, they argue, if Jesus is arriving tomorrow?

American fundamentalists are a headache, a thorn in flesh of the *bien-pensant* liberals, the subject of bemused concern to Old Europeans who have experienced too many real catastrophes to yearn for Armageddon. Whatever spiritual benefits individuals may have gained by taking Jesus as their personal saviour, the apocalyptic fantasies harboured by born-again Christians have a negative effect on public policy. Because of its impact on the environment and its baleful role in the Middle East, America's religiosity is a problem.

But the solution is also American. The constitutional separation of church and state is as fundamental to American democracy as the Bible is to fundamentalists. The hard line preached by televangelists such as Falwell and Robertson is protected by the First Amendment, but it is also limited by it. Though fundamentalists can influence policy, they cannot control it. The same considerations apply, by and large, to fundamentalists in Israel, Sri Lanka, and India, who are constrained by the pluralistic and democratic political systems in which they operate.

The Islamic situation is different, because for historical and sociological reasons too complex to explain in this book, very few Muslim political cultures have developed along democratic lines. In their ruthless drive to power, Islamists have succeeded in taking control of the state temporarily in Sudan, Pakistan, and Afghanistan and permanently in Saudi Arabia and (under different sectarian colours) in Iran. Where the Islamist tide has receded or been checked (as in Pakistan, Egypt, and Algeria), it has been ruthless action by the military rather than the constraints of democratic institutions that have protected secular government. The association of religious pluralism and secularism with militarism (as in Syria, Pakistan, and Turkey) rather than with democracy has been an important element in the Islamist rhetorical armoury.

Where the military governs along secular lines, as in Algeria or in Turkey during periods of army intervention, Islamists can plausibly appeal to democratic feelings. But where Islamists actually hold power, as in Iran, they resist democratic progress as being contrary to the will of God. There are ways out of this vicious spiral, but they require fine political tuning. An example is offered by Turkey, where in order to win democratically Islamists have had to abandon their more strident demands for 're-Islamizing' society.

Despite these very real problems, the call for freedom, even when polluted by the suspicion that it is being exploited by commercial interests, still runs with the grain of popular aspirations. Islamism, like other fundamentalisms, works best in opposition. In power it proves no less susceptible to corruption or manipulation than the ideologies and systems it seeks to supplant. For the foreseeable future, Muslim nationalists will doubtless continue to resist American global hegemony, along with Russian imperialism in Transcaucasia and the Israeli subjugation of Palestine. But in other respects, the power of modern technology may be working in America's direction. In the age of satellite broadcasting and the internet, pluralism and diversity of choice are no longer aspirations. They are dynamic realities with which believers of all traditions are having to contend.

References

Chapter 1

Bruce B. Lawrence, *Defenders of God* (San Francisco: Harper and Row, 1989)

Anthony Kenny (ed.), *The Wittgenstein Reader* (Oxford: Blackwell, 1994)

Paul Boyer, *When Time Shall Be No More: Prophesy Belief in Modern American Culture* (Cambridge, Mass.: Harvard Belknap Press, 1992)

Martin Marty, 'The Fundamentals of Fundamentalism', in Lawrence Kaplan (ed.), *Fundamentalism in Comparative Perspective* (Amherst, Mass.: University of Massachusetts Press, 1992)

Martin E. Marty and R. Scott Appleby, *Accounting for Fundamentalisms* (The Fundamentalism Project, vol. 4, Chicago: Chicago University Press, 1995)

Martin E. Marty and R. Scott Appleby, *The Glory and the Power* (Boston: Beacon Press, 1992)

Garry Wills, *Under God: Religion and American Politics* (New York: Simon and Schuster, 1990)

Adolf Hitler, speech 22 August 1939, cited in Ernst Nolte, *Three Faces of Fascism* (New York: Mentor, 1969)

Vincent Crapanzano, *Serving the Word: Literalism in America from the Pulpit to the Bench* (New York: The New Press, 2000)

Henry Morris, *The Remarkable Birth of Planet Earth* (San Diego: Institute of Creation Science, 1986)

Philip Kitcher, *Abusing Science: The Case against Creationism* (Cambridge, Mass.: MIT Press, 1982)

Chapter 2

al-Jabarti, Abd al-Rahman, *Napoleon in Egypt: al-Jabarti's Chronicle of the French Occupation 1798*, tr. Shmuel Moreh (Princeton: Markus Weiner, 1997)

Sayyid Qutb, *Fi Zilal al-Quran* (Beirut: Dar al-Shuruq, 1981), vol. 1, cited by Youssef M. Choueiri, *Islamic Fundamentalism* (Boston: Twayne, 1990)

Don Cupitt, *The Sea of Faith* (London: BBC, 1984)

Sayyid Abu Ala Mawdudi, *The Religion of Truth* (Lahore: Islamic Publications, 1967)

Clifford Geertz, cited in Martin E. Marty, 'The Fundamentals of Fundamentalism', in Lawrence Kaplan (ed.), *Fundamentalism in Comparative Perspective* (Amherst, Mass.: University of Massachusetts Press, 1992)

Pierre Bayle, cited in Ernst Cassirier, *The Philosophy of the Enlightenment*, tr. Fritz C. A. Koelln and James P. Pettegrove (Princeton: Princeton University Press, 1951)

Will Herberg, *Protestant, Catholic, Jew, an Essay in American Religious Sociology* (New York: Anchor Books, 1960)

Steve Bruce, 'Revelations: The Future of the New Christian Right', in Lawrence Kaplan (ed.), *Fundamentalism in Comparative Perspective* (Amherst, Mass.: University of Massachusetts Press, 1992)

Chapter 3

James Barr, *Fundamentalism* (Philadelphia: Westminster Press, 1978)

Vincent Crapanzano, *Serving the Word: Literalism in America from the Pulpit to the Bench* (New York: The New Press, 2000)

Richard Elliot Friedman, *Who Wrote the Bible?* (New York: Harper and Row, 1987)

Maurice Bucaille, *The Bible, the Qur'an and Science*, tr. Alastair D. Pannell and the author (Indianapolis: American Trust Publications, 1979)

Koran 22: 5

John A. Coleman, 'Catholic Integralism as a Fundamentalism', in
Lawrence Kaplan (ed.), *Fundamentalism in Comparative Perspective*
(Amherst, Mass.: University of Massachusetts Press, 1992)

Richard Bell and Montgomery Watt, *Introduction to the Quran*
(Edinburgh: Edinburgh University Press, 1977)

Stephen R. Humphreys, *Islamic History: A Framework for Inquiry*
(Princeton: Princeton University Press, 1991)

John Wansbrough, *Quranic Studies: Sources and Methods of Scriptural
Interpretation* (Oxford: Oxford University Press, 1977)

Gerald Hawting, *The Idea of Idolatry and the Emergence of Islam:
From Polemic to History* (Cambridge: Cambridge University Press,
1999)

Karen Armstrong, *The Battle for God: Fundamentalism in Judaism,
Christianity and Islam* (London: Harper Collins, 2000)

Anthony Giddens, *The Consequences of Modernity* (Stanford, CA:
Stanford University Press, 1990)

Pascal Boyer, *Religion Explained: The Human Instincts that Fashion
Gods, Spirits and Ancestors* (London: Vintage, 2002)

Niels C. Nielson, Jr, *Fundamentalism, Mythos, and World Religions*
(Albany, NY: SUNY Press, 1993)

Kathleen Raine, *Blake and the New Age* (London: Allen and Unwin,
1979)

Yehoshafat Harkabi, *Israel's Fateful Decisions* (London: I. B. Tauris,
1988)

Ian Lustick, *For the Land and the Lord: Jewish Fundamentalism in
Israel* (New York: Council on Foreign Relations, 1988)

Chapter 4

John Stratton Hawley (ed.), *Fundamentalism and Gender* (New York:
Oxford University Press, 1994)

Sakuntala Narasimhan, *Sati: A Study of Widow Burning in India* (New
Delhi: HarperCollins, 1998)

Martin Riesebrodt, *Pious Passion – The Emergence of Modern
Fundamentalism in the United States and Iran*, tr. Don Renau
(Berkeley: University of California Press, 1993)

Jorge E. Maldonado, 'Building "Fundamentalism" from the Family in

Latin America', in Martin E. Marty and R. Scott Appleby (eds), *Fundamentalism and Society* (Chicago: University of Chicago Press, 1993)

Valentine M. Moghadam, 'Fundamentalism and the Woman Question in Afghanistan', in Lawrence Kaplan (ed.), *Fundamentalism in Comparative Perspective* (Amherst, Mass.: University of Massachusetts Press, 1992)

Frances Fitzgerald, *Cities on a Hill* (New York: Simon and Schuster, 1986)

Anita Weiss, in Akbar S. Ahmed and Hastings Donnan (eds), *Islam, Globalization and Postmodernity* (London: Routledge, 1994)

Chapter 5

Steve Brower, Paul Gifford, and Susan D. Rose, *Exporting the American Gospel* (New York and London: Routledge, 1998)

Pat Robertson, *The Turning Tide: The Fall of Liberalism and the Rise of Common Sense* (Dallas: World Publishing, 1993)

Sayyid Abu Ala Mawdudi, *The Religion of Truth* (Lahore: Islamic Publications, 1967)

Albert Hourani, *A History of the Arab Peoples* (London: Faber, 2002)

Mark Juergensmeyer, *The New Cold War? Religious Nationalism Confronts the Secular State* (Berkeley: University of California Press, 1993)

Laura Guazzone (ed.), *The Islamist Dilemma: The Political Role of Islamist Movements in the Contemporary Arab World* (Reading: Ithaca Press, 1995)

Gilles Kepel, *Jihad: The Trail of Political Islam* (London: I. B. Tauris, 2002)

Chapter 6

Anthony D. Smith, *Chosen Peoples: Sacred Foundations of National Identity* (Oxford: Oxford University Press, 2004)

Sybil Sheridan, 'Judaism', in Jean Holm and John Bowker (eds), *Myth and History* (London: Pinter, 1994)

Rudolf Bultmann, *History and Eschatology* (Edinburgh: Edinburgh University Press, 1957)

Ian Lustick, *For the Land and the Lord: Jewish Fundamentalism in Israel* (New York: Council on Foreign Relations, 1988)

Mark Juergensmeyer, *Terror in the Mind of God: The Global Rise of Religious Violence* (Berkeley: University of California Press, 2000)

Jehoshafat Harkabi, *Israeli's Fateful Decisions* (London: I. B. Tauris, 1988)

Steve Bruce, *Fundamentalism* (Cambridge: Polity Press, 2000)

Daniel Gold, 'Organised Hinduisms', in Martin E. Marty and R. Scott Appleby (eds), *Fundamentalisms Observed* (Chicago: University of Chicago Press, 1991)

Sunil Khilnani, *The Idea of India* (London: Hamish Hamilton, 1997)

T. N. Madan, 'The Double-Edged Sword: Fundamentalism and the Sikh Religious Tradition', in Marty and Appleby, *Fundamentalisms Observed*

Donald K. Swearer, 'Fundamentalist Movements in Theraveda Buddhism', in Marty and Appleby, *Fundamentalisms Observed*

S. N. Eisenstadt, *Fundamentalism, Sectarianism and Revolution* (Cambridge: Cambridge University Press, 2000)

Chapter 7

Harvey Cox, *The Secular City: Secularization and Urbanization in Theological Perspective* (New York: Macmillan, 1990)

Anthony Giddens, *The Consequnces of Modernity* (Stanford, CA: Stanford University Press, 1990)

Jeff Haynes, 'Religion, Secularization, and Politics: A Postmodern Conspectus', *Third World Quarterly*, 18(4), 1997

Anson Shupe and Jeffrey K. Hadden, 'Is There Such a Thing as Global Fundamentalism?', in Anson Shupe and Jeffrey K. Hadden (eds), *Secularization and Fundamentalism Reconsidered* (New York: Paragon House, 1989)

Steve Bruce, *The Rise and Fall of the New Christian Right* (Oxford: Clarendon Press, 1988)

Malise Ruthven, *A Fury for God: The Islamist Attack on America* (London: Granta, 2002)

Further reading

Five volumes of essays by scholars from different disciplines may be found in the path-breaking series produced by the Fundamentalism Project between 1991 and 1996 under the auspices of the American Academy of Sciences and the University of Chicago. Edited by Martin E. Marty and R. Scott Appleby, they are: vol. 1, *Fundamentalisms Observed* (1991); vol. 2, *Fundamentalisms and Society* (1993); vol. 3, *Fundamentalisms and the State* (1993); vol. 4, *Accounting for Fundamentalisms* (1995); vol. 5, *Fundamentalisms Comprehended* (1996), all published by the University of Chicago Press. A much more accessible single-volume version based on three television documentaries produced in association with the Fundamentalism Project is Marty and Appleby's *The Glory and the Power* (Boston: Beacon Press, 1992).

An essay that broadens discussion of the F-word to embrace doctrinaire monetarism, Marxism, anti-Marxism, neoconservatism, Euroscepticism, and other political trends in the context of theoretical debates about modernism and postmodernism, is Stuart Sims' *Fundamentalist World: The New Dark Age of Dogma* (Cambridge: Icon, 2004). Other comparative studies include: Karen Armstrong, *The Battle for God – Fundamentalism in Judaism, Christianity and Islam* (London: HarperCollins, 2000); Steve Bruce, *Fundamentalism* (Cambridge: Polity Press, 2000); Lionel Caplan (ed.), *Studies in Religious Fundamentalism* (Albany, NY: SUNY Press, 1987); Mark

Juergensmeyer, *The New Cold War? Religious Nationalism Confronts the Secular State* (Berkeley: University of California Press, 1993) and *Terror in the Mind of God – The Global Rise of Religious Violence* (Berkeley: University of California Press, 2001); Lawrence Kaplan (ed.), *Fundamentalism in Comparative Perspective* (Amherst, MA: University of Massachusetts Press, 1992); Gilles Kepel, *The Revenge of God: The Resurgence of Islam, Christianity and Judaism in the Modern World*, tr. Alan Braley (Cambridge: Polity Press, 1994); Bruce Lawrence, *Defenders of God: The Fundamentalist Revolt against the Modern Age* (San Francisco: Harper and Row, 1990); Martin Riesebrodt, *Pious Passion – The Emergence of Modern Fundamentalism in the United States and Iran*, tr. Don Renau (Berkeley: University of California Press, 1993).

The relationships between fundamentalisms and gender are explored in: Brenda Brasher, *Godly Women: Fundamentalism and Female Power* (New Brunswick, NJ: Rutgers University Press, 1998); Judy Brink and Joan Mencher (eds), *Mixed Blessings: Gender and Religious Fundamentalisms Cross Culturally* (London/New York: Routledge, 1997); Betty A. DeBerg, *Ungodly Women: Gender and the First Wave of American Fundamentalism* (Minneapolis: Fortress Press, 1990); John Stratton Hawley (ed.), *Fundamentalism and Gender* (Oxford: Oxford University Press, 1994); and Sakuntala Narasimhan, *Sati: A Study of Widow Burning in India* (New Delhi: HarperCollins, 1998).

Issues of literalism and textual inerrancy are addressed in James Barr, *Fundamentalism* (Philadelphia: Westminster Press, 1978) and Vincent Crapanzano, *Serving the Word: Literalism in America from the Pulpit to the Bench* (New York: The New Press, 2000).

Most of the other studies consulted for this book deal with fundamentalisms in separate religious or political contexts. Sources for Jewish fundamentalism include David Landau, *Piety and Power: The World of Jewish Fundamentalism* (London: Secker and Warburg, 1994) and Ian Lustick, *For the Land and the Lord: Jewish Fundamentalism in Israel* (New York: Council for Foreign Relations, 1988). The Christian variants are examined in Nancy Tatom Ammerman, *Bible Believers: Fundamentalists in the Modern World* (New Brunswick: Rutgers University Press, 1987); Paul Boyer, *When Time Shall Be No More: Prophesy Belief in Modern American Culture* (Cambridge, MA: Harvard Belknap Press, 1991); Steve Bruce, *The Rise and Fall of the New Christian Right: Conservative Protestant Politics in America 1978–1988* (Oxford: Clarendon Press, 1988); Susan F. Harding, *The Book of Jerry Falwell* (Princeton: Princeton University Press, 2000); and Gary Wills, *Under God: Religion and American Politics* (New York: Simon and Schuster, 1990). The burgeoning scholarly literature on Islamic fundamentalism includes Akbar S. Ahmed and Hastings Donnan (eds), *Islam, Globalization and Postmodernity* (London: Routledge, 1996); John Esposito (ed.), *Voices of Resurgent Islam* (New York: Oxford University Press, 1983); Laura Guazzone (ed.), *The Islamist Dilemma: The Political Role of Islamist Movements in the Contemporary Arab World* (Reading: Ithaca Press, 1995); Johannes J. G. Jansen, *The Neglected Duty: The Creed of Sadat's Assassins and Islamic Resurgence in the Middle East* (New York: Macmillan, 1986); Gilles Kepel, *The Prophet and Pharaoh: Muslim Extremism in Egypt*, tr. Jon Rothschild (London: Saqi Books, 1990), *Jihad: The Trail of Political Islam* (London: I. B. Tauris, 2002), and *The War for Muslim Minds: Islam and the West*, tr. Pascale Ghazaleh (Cambridge, MA: Harvard University Press, 2004); Olivier Roy, *The Failure of Political Islam* (London: I. B. Tauris, 1994) and *Globalized Islam: The Search for a New Ummah* (London: I. B. Tauris, 2004); and Malise Ruthven, *A Fury for God: The Islamist Attack on America* (London: Granta Books, 2003).

Index

Index

Fundamentalism

Expand your collection of
VERY SHORT INTRODUCTIONS

Visit the
VERY SHORT INTRODUCTIONS
Web site

www.oup.co.uk/vsi

➤ **Information** about all published titles

➤ News of **forthcoming books**

➤ **Extracts** from the books, including titles not yet published

➤ **Reviews** and views

➤ **Links** to other **web sites** and main OUP web page

➤ Information about **VSIs in translation**

➤ **Contact** the editors

➤ **Order** other **VSIs** on-line

ANIMAL RIGHTS
A Very Short Introduction
David DeGrazia

Do animals have moral rights? If so, what does this mean?
What sorts of mental lives do animals have, and how
should we understand their welfare? After putting forward
answers to these questions, David DeGrazia explores the
implications for how we treat animals in connection with
our diet, zoos, and research.

'This is an ideal introduction to the topic. David DeGrazia
does a superb job of bringing all the key issues together
in a balanced way, in a volume that is both short and very
readable.'

Peter Singer, Princeton University

'Historically aware, philosophically sensitive, and with
many well-chosen examples, this book would be hard to
beat as a philosophical introduction to animal rights.'

Roger Crisp, Oxford University

www.oup.co.uk/isbn/0-19-285360-0

SOCIAL AND CULTURAL ANTHROPOLOGY
A Very Short Introduction

John Monaghan and Peter Just

'If you want to know what anthropology *is*, look at what anthropologists *do*.'

This Very Short Introduction to Social and Cultural Anthropology combines an accessible account of some of the discipline's guiding principles and methodology with abundant examples and illustrations of anthropologists at work.

Peter Just and John Monaghan begin by discussing anthropology's most important contributions to modern thought: its investigation of culture as a distinctly 'human' characteristic, its doctrine of cultural relativism, and its methodology of fieldwork and ethnography. They then examine specific ways in which social and cultural anthropology have advanced our understanding of human society and culture, drawing on examples from their own fieldwork. The book ends with an assessment of anthropology's present position, and a look forward to its likely future.

www.oup.co.uk/vsi/anthropology

ISLAM
A Very Short Introduction
Malise Ruthven

Islam features widely in the news, often in its most militant versions, but few people in the non-Muslim world really understand the nature of Islam.

Malise Ruthven's Very Short Introduction contains essential insights into issues such as why Islam has such major divisions between movements such as the Shi'ites, the Sunnis, and the Wahhabis, and the central import-ance of the Shar'ia (Islamic law) in Islamic life. It also offers fresh perspectives on contemporary questions: Why is the greatest 'Jihad' (holy war) now against the enimies of Islam, rather than the struggle against evil? Can women find fulfilment in Islamic societies? How must Islam adapt as it confronts the modern world?

> 'Malise Ruthven's book answers the urgent need for an introduction to Islam. ... He addresses major issues with clarity and directness, engages dispassionately with the disparate stereotypes and polemics on the subject, and guides the reader surely through urgent debates about fundamentalism.'
>
> **Michael Gilsenan, New York University**

www.oup.co.uk/vsi/islam

HINDUISM
A Very Short Introduction
Kim Knott

Hinduism is practised by eighty per cent of India's population, and by thirty million people outside India. In this Very Short Introduction, Kim Knott combines a succinct and authoritative overview of a major religion with an analysis of the challenges facing it in the twentieth century. She discusses key preoccupations of Hinduism such as the centrality of the *Veda* as religious texts, the role of brahmins, gurus, and storytellers in the transmission of divine truths, and the importance of epics such as the *Ramayana*. Issues such as the place of women and *dalits* (untouchables) in contemporary society are also addressed, making this book stimulating reading for Hindus and non-Hindus alike.

> 'This book is instantly accessible in its approach without being in any way condescending or an oversimplification.'
>
> **Julia Leslie, School of Oriental and African Studies, London**

> 'very readable and certainly most helpful, with a new and original perspective conveyed in a succinct introductory style'
>
> **Ursula King, University of Bristol**

www.oup.co.uk/vsi/hinduism

THE BIBLE
A Very Short Introduction
John Riches

It is sometimes said that the Bible is one of the most unread books in the world, yet it has been a major force in the development of Western culture and continues to exert an enormous influence over many people's lives. This Very Short Introduction looks at the importance accorded to the Bible by different communities and cultures and attempts to explain why it has generated such a rich variety of uses and interpretations. It explores how the Bible was written, the development of the canon, the role of Biblical criticism, the appropriation of the Bible in high and popular culture, and its use for political ends.

'John Riches' clear and lively Very Short Introduction offers a distinctive approach to the Bible ... a distinguished addition to the series.'
Christopher Rowland, University of Oxford

'Short in length, but not in substance, nor in interest. A fascinating introduction both to the way in which the Bible came to be what it is, and to what it means and has meant for believers.'
Joel Marcus, Boston University

www.oup.co.uk/vsi/bible

THE KORAN
A Very Short Introduction
Michael Cook

The Koran has constituted a remarkably resilient core of identity and continuity for a religious tradition that is now in its fifteenth century. In this Very Short Introduction, Michael Cook provides a lucid and direct account of the significance of the Koran both in the modern world and in that of traditional Islam. He gives vivid accounts of its role in Muslim civilization, and compares it to other scriptures and classics of the historic cultures of Eurasia.

> 'Professor Cook's book is informative, witty, and rich with insight. The author firmly places the Koran within its broader context, lending his treatment depth and vigour.'
> **Mohamed Mahmoud, Tufts University**

> 'This is a brilliant work of lucid scholarship and well-designed synthesis.'
> **Ian Netton, University of Leeds**

www.oup.co.uk/vsi/koran

POSTMODERNISM
A Very Short Introduction
Christopher Butler

Postmodernism has become the buzzword of
contemporary society over the last decade. But how can it
be defined? In this Very Short Introduction Christopher
Butler lithely challenges and explores the key ideas of
postmodernism, and their engagement with literature, the
visual arts, film, architecture, and music. He treats artists,
intellectuals, critics, and social scientists 'as if they were all
members of a loosely constituted and quarrelsome
political party' – a party which includes such members as
Jacques Derrida, Salman Rushdie, Thomas Pynchon,
David Bowie, and Micheal Craig-Martin – creating a vastly
entertaining framework in which to unravel the mysteries
of the 'postmodern condition', from the politicizing of
museum culture to the cult of the politically correct.

> 'a preeminently sane, lucid, and concise statement about
> the central issues, the key examples, and the notorious
> derilections of postmodernism. I feel a fresh wind blowing
> away the miasma coiling around the topic.'
>
> **Ihab Hassan, University of Wisconsin, Milwaukee**

www.oup.co.uk/isbn/0-19-280239-9